M000249818

A WEAPON IN HIS HAND

Special Forces To Royal Assignment

By Keir Tayler

with Janet Rodriguez

Dedication

For Callie, my wife,
and our three children:
Jenni, Simon and Lisa

Keir Tayler

P | +27 12 991 3057
C | +27 83 621 5347
F | +27 12 991 3057
E | keir@handinhand.co.za

Hand In Hand International
KeirTayler.com

Ordering: Books are available from KeirTayler.com.
US Wholesale / Bulk orders: contact the publisher

Published: ArtiFactInk | PO Box 717, Camino CA 95709, USA | ArtiFactInk.com
            Phone: (US +) 530-621-4224 | Book design: Martha Dayton

Janet Rodriguez is a freelance writer and blogger living in Northern California. Follow her on twitter @brazenprincess or at brazenprincess.com.

Cover Art & Website: Simon Tayler - hykano.com
Sword photo: iStock.com - used by permission

Priting: First Edition   ISBN # 978-0-9963505-0-1
Library of Congress Control Number: 2015940564

TABLE OF CONTENTS

Finally, be strong in the Lord and in the strength of His might. Put on the full armor of God, so that you will be able to stand firm against the schemes of the devil. For our struggle is not against flesh and blood, but against the rulers, against the powers, against the world forces of this darkness, against the spiritual forces of wickedness in the heavenly places. Therefore, take up the full armor of God, so that you will be able to resist in the evil day, and having done everything, to stand firm. Stand firm therefore, HAVING GIRDED YOUR LOINS WITH TRUTH, and HAVING PUT ON THE BREASTPLATE OF RIGHTEOUSNESS, and having shod YOUR FEET WITH THE PREPARATION OF THE GOSPEL OF PEACE; in addition to all, taking up the shield of faith with which you will be able to extinguish all the flaming arrows of the evil one. And take THE HELMET OF SALVATION, and the sword of the Spirit, which is the word of God. With all prayer and petition pray at all times in the Spirit, and with this in view, be on the alert with all perseverance and petition for all the saints, and pray on my behalf, that utterance may be given to me in the opening of my mouth, to make known with boldness the mystery of the gospel, for which I am an ambassador in chains; that in proclaiming it I may speak boldly, as I ought to speak.

Ephesians 6: 10-20
(NASB)

PROLOGUE:

A WORD FROM CALLIE

Only, as the Lord has assigned to each one,
as God has called each, in this manner let him walk.
And so I direct in all the churches.

1 Corinthians 7:17

What you are about to read is our story, or part of it anyway. When I first met Keir he seemed to be one of the largest men I had ever met. I remember looking into his eyes and seeing great strength (which was attractive to me) but also sincerity and gentleness. People later called him the 'gentle giant' which is an accurate description – he is a man of impressive size, but he usually disarms people with his compassion.

I must say that God's calling on us has proven itself to be genuine and eternal - a huge blessing to walk in. Both Keir and I responded to this call; both of us agreed to trust God. I was not just "Callie the wife" or "Callie the tag-along". I would never have been able to walk this out for thirty-five years unless God had spoken to me as well. Keir is a man of incredible faith, a man who trusts God when everything around us is crumbling to bits – I've seen this time and time again. Because of this, I've learned to trust Keir as he trusts God.

Before I could be sure about all of this, God had to speak to me Himself. I didn't want to go to America and attend Christ for the Nations Institute, a Bible school that Keir admired. Instead of forcing me, Keir accepted my opinion as a sign that it wasn't the right time to pursue this direction. I was on my way home from a women's Bible study when God arrested me. He said, 'If you will be obedient to Keir and go to Christ for the Nations then Keir can be obedient to me. I will call you both into this ministry and protect you all the way.'

That word has kept me going all of these years.

Over the years, that word has been tested. Once, when our children were small, we were burgled during an already 'lean' financial time. We were without a car as ours had just broken down and we couldn't afford the repairs for it, so it was sitting in our garage. Then came the burglary and quite a few of our things were taken. Keir was able to apprehend the scoundrels by running down the road and catching them. When the police came around to take the burglars into custody, they took our statements, thanked us and left. That was that. About a month later, the police came back to us (which was unheard of!), telling Keir that he was entitled to a cash reward for catching the thieves. They gave him the exact amount that we needed to fix our car! This is just one example of how God has provided for us in creative ways.

Keir and I have now been married for forty years. We have three children and nine grandchildren and our lives are very rich! I have learned to trust God with Keir and I have also learned to relax. When Keir hears God and trusts Him, it's good for all of us. So my part in our journey has mainly been finding rest in God and I'm grateful that His mercy has been strong and unwavering.

I have learned to never take things for granted with God. I wake up each day and say, 'God what do you have for us today? How can we walk with you today?' As I live each day in trust, I am amazed at how God moves. Each day He amazes me and I live my life in a grateful place.

I pray that as you read this you will be touched by the grace of God. I pray that our story inspires you to trust in Him completely, because He cares for you.

Callie Tayler

1

FLESH AND BLOOD

"For our struggle is not against flesh and blood, but against the rulers, against the powers, against the world forces of this darkness, against the spiritual forces of wickedness in the heavenly places."

Ephesians 6:12 NASB

On a warm spring day in 1999, I decided to go to the movies to see *Saving Private Ryan*, an American film that had just been released in South Africa. I went alone, as none of my friends could accompany me. I arrived at the cinema, paid for a matinee show and found a single seat in the sparsely populated theatre.

I had heard a lot about this epic war film, especially the first twenty minutes and its realistic depiction of the Normandy invasion by the Allied Forces. Having been a soldier, I am usually interested in (and inspired by) any movie that depicts a soldier giving everything to a battle, regardless of the cost.

After settling into my seat, the cinema darkened and the screen lit up with scenes from upcoming features. I waited, relaxed and expectant for the feature film to start. The opening scene of Saving Private Ryan begins with an elderly man surrounded by his family visiting a cemetery. They approach a field of crosses, and the elderly man falls to his knees in front of one (presumably that of someone he knew well), tears streaming down his face. Suddenly, the film transitions and transports us to Omaha Beach – the Allied invasion of 1944.

I watched as naval transports carrying fresh soldiers approached the beach to assemble strategically for the invasion. Suddenly, a vicious battle scene began. The miracle of digital surround sound filled the room with realistic sounds of war: gunfire on the screen became bullets flying around my head. All around me were the snap and pop sounds of explosives; I nearly dived for cover.

My heart kicked into red-alert, thumping wildly in my chest. Blood rushed from my chest to my neck with great force. My breath was sharp and shallow and my body went rigid with alarm. I realized I was gripping the armrests of my chair with sweaty palms. Panic-stricken, I looked around.

I was at the movies.

The wall at the end of the row of empty seats was covered in red velvet wallpaper; there was a screen in front of me. I forced my brain to process, despite the noise. I forced myself to accept that I was not being fired at; I wasn't in battle, I didn't have the enemy charging at me. I breathed in through my nose - there was no smell of blood or of flesh burning. I sat there in my seat and willed my heartbeat to return to normal. I wanted to do it; I had to - as a soldier. I forced myself to watch what I had paid to see, despite the fear that gripped me.

I am watching a movie, I said, over and over again. *I am watching a movie.*

I am only watching a movie.

———

I experienced quite a flashback that afternoon in the cinema. It triggered a memory of the Nyadzonya Raid, an invasion that I was a part of – one that changed my life.

In July of 1976 I was twenty-seven years old, dividing my time be-tween the army and a civilian job at the histopathology laboratory in Borrowdale Road, Salisbury. Rabies had been spreading like wildfire into Rhodesia (now Zimbabwe); many infected dogs, cattle and other animals were straying in from Mozambique. In its final stages, the disease causes infected animals to become vicious and attack people without provocation. Rabid dogs had attacked many who lived along the border.

My job at the lab involved preparing slices of brain tissue from these affected animals, preserving them and then studying them under an ultraviolet microscope. Tissues that tested positive for rabies meant that I would have to alert the people who had been bitten to this. Since the medical treatment that followed proved to be quite traumatic for some patients, this was not an easy job. Despite its stress, my position in the lab suited me. I enjoyed working with detail and seemed drawn to the medical side of the work; I was in great demand as the rabies threat was increasing. Yet, this wasn't my identity. I was Keir the soldier - my real passion was Special Forces training.

My homeland, Rhodesia, was engaged in a civil war, one whose outcome would determine the future of our nation. I had volunteered for the Special Forces regiment of the Rhodesian Army: the Selous Scouts, men who were the bravest of the brave. We would march into any battle as long as it was against terrorism. We were seasoned warriors, unafraid of the enemy. Like most soldiers involved in an emotionally charged civil war, I believed in what we were doing. I was convinced that our side was fighting for the ideals that would sustain and benefit Rhodesia and its entire population.

Since we trained constantly, the idea that I must be ready at any moment was constantly reinforced. I took it seriously, becoming proficient in weapons and machinery. I learned quickly and became quite skilled among my peers: I was ready to attack terrorists who were threatening Rhodesia's way of life.

One night I came home from the clinic and found a note attached to the front door of my cottage, 'requesting' that I report to the camp early the next morning. I knew what this meant: I had been called up to combat. Callie was pregnant with our first child and naturally I didn't want to leave her. Nevertheless, duty called and at six the next morning Callie dropped me off at the camp and we said goodbye to one another.

As I entered the bustling base I greeted my band of brothers – the 'belted and bereted' Selous Scouts who were all ready for any action, anytime. In the middle of our camp, parked in full view, was the Unimog vehicle that I had been training on for the last month. Attached to it was an enormous weapon called a Hispano 20mm: a cannon that we had been learning to fire. Originally designed as an aircraft weapon for strafing trains, it discharged large amounts of ammunition. As the 'number two man' on the Hispano 20mm it was my job to make sure the belt of ammunition discharged smoothly without jamming or stoppages. The sight of it made me feel sure that there was a serious battle ahead.

 The team I worked with knew that our vehicle was not ready to be taken into battle. That morning we prepared it to be the fighting machine it was supposed to be; now and then speculating on what we would be doing with it. We were also outfitted with full weapons: 12.7mm caliber machine guns, AK- 47s with 50mm caliber Brownings, mounted side by side.

That afternoon we drove the vehicle to the eastern part of the country to meet up with the other troops who were already staged there. Hidden under the trees, protected from satellite detection, we were briefed about our mission. The captain addressed us with sober authority.

'Tomorrow morning, just after eight o'clock, we will storm into a terrorist training camp in Mozambique. Our intelligence has found the location and our orders are to attack it.'

He pulled out a map of the area, placed it against the vehicle and in the setting sun he began to tell us our mission strategy. I remember all of us sitting around and listening to him; we looked like lads sitting on the grass and rocks, paying close attention to a schoolteacher who was explaining a lesson.

 'Three weeks ago we received information that there are roughly a thousand terrorists-in-training at this particular camp. At eight in the morning they have roll call where they will all line up and stand at attention. Each terrorist will be present, receiving his orders for the day.'

He showed us the entry points; how we would go into the camp with an element of surprize. We would dress just like them, in their camouflage. The white Scouts were instructed to darken their skin with oil paste and to leave no white flesh exposed; this way they would think we were with them (my fellow Selous Scouts with dark skins were ready as they were). We'd drive into the camp just after muster parade and address the whole crowd with a microphone and have the enlisted men surrender and line up quietly. The officers would be assembled and taken into a boma where they would be captured and we would get information from them. While this was happening, we were all to shoot the enlisted men; killing them where they were standing. We would continue on to a second camp and do the very same thing. We were told we would blow-up the bridges behind us so that we could not be followed. After the second camp was destroyed, we were told that we'd have to find our way out of the country, going west through the bush until we were no longer in Mozambique.

When we heard these orders, we all were shocked. I remember finding a piece of corrugated iron lying in the field that night and climbing under it, just so I could separate myself from this horrific reality. I wasn't expecting this; I didn't see myself volunteering for this kind of mission. I wondered that night if I would ever see Callie or my home again; extreme fear filled me.

Nevertheless, at one o'clock in the morning, I joined my band of brothers and we assembled to begin the journey into Mozambique. I was programmed to do whatever I was told to do, despite the fear and the questions. The journey was long and very intense; hardly anyone spoke. It was a somber time.

At eight o'clock we stopped to do a final check. Once it had been completed, we proceeded. I remember looking around and noticing that it was a beautiful day; the sky was blue and clear and the sun was shining. Under any other circumstances, it would have been a perfect day.

When we arrived at the camp, we crashed through its crude barrier and took positions in a semi-circle surrounding it. The camp itself had a massive river running through it, supposedly infested with crocodiles. We were betting that most of the enemy couldn't swim; and the ones who could, might be too afraid. On one side of the camp was a steep cliff that our commanding officers said would prevent them from escaping. Our vehicles surrounded all other sides.

I could tell immediately that the information we had been given was incorrect. This was no camp of a thousand soldiers; there were over five thousand men there and, at the sight of us they started cheering. They charged toward us, dancing and singing, not fearing bloodshed or death. With their fists, they pumped the air, chanting 'Z! Z! Z!' for Zimbabwe. They came upon us quickly, five thousand men chanting, singing and jumping up and down. We were sitting in the vehicle when they slowly started realizing that things weren't as they appeared; we were the enemy. The soldiers in my vehicle were frozen; we all realized Plan A was nonexistent; Plan B involved that massive 20mm cannon sitting in the middle of the vehicle between us. I remember hearing gunfire ring out and then we began firing the

Hispano 20–mill, each round a high-explosive missile.

The carnage was instant and graphic; I saw bodies exploding every-where in front of me. Bits of intestines and limbs flew everywhere; a few landed next to me in a tree. The cacophony was deafening and the air was filled with a moist stench. I was inhaling cordite fumes tainted with vaporized blood. My uniform was suddenly covered in a pinkish film, sprayed everywhere from the bloodbath before us. Adrenaline pumping and in chaotic hell, I suddenly felt a searing pain rip through my legs and felt a burning deep in my bones: I had been shot.

I looked down and saw a fountain of blood spurting out of my right thigh. My left knee was completely torn open. I put my gloved hand into my torn camo denims to feel for my kneecap; it was still there. If I had been shot in a femoral artery, I knew I was going to bleed to death within two minutes.

Instantly, my heart was filled with doubt and fear. Where would I go once I died? I knew I hadn't lived the life of a Christian; I wasn't a good person at all. In that moment, I remembered my Dad reading the Bible to me when I was six or seven years old; I knew the most important thing was what Jesus had said on the cross: 'Into your hands I commit my Spirit.' I thought: As I die, I'll say the same thing. Religion or Christianity didn't factor in. I was a dying man - it was all useless now.

In the midst of all the chaos around me, with blood gushing from my thigh, I shouted, 'Lord, if you want my life, you can have it!' Instantly, a brilliant light surrounded me. The pain, the fear, the terror of death and the carnage around me left. I was so captivated by that light that I could see or feel nothing else. There was a Presence, an extreme peace accompanied by what seemed to be vaporized droplets of oil, each drop emitting light. It was almost tangible. Time stood still; I could see people running past me in slow motion. I looked down at my leg and only a small trickle of blood was escaping, slowly. The presence of God was all around, enveloping me in an incredible feeling of awe. Everything was brand new around me, even the dusty camouflage and the AK-47 I held in my hands. I was watching every-thing going on around me; I was part of it but not part of it. I was part of something greater and even more powerful. I was in a situa-tion that required the greatest amount of concern but I was suddenly not worried. It was the first time that I realized there really was a God. I had prayed the prayer of surrender and I meant it. I wasn't expecting to live; but I now knew there was a God and He was surrounding me.

I managed to climb off the bench I had been sitting on and moved to the back of the vehicle to load my weapon. At that point, the brilliant light of God seemed to dim, and regular daylight was again around me. The machine gunner was working the gun, and the activity of war continued.

We were soon moving, racing out of the camp and into a clearing. The vehicle jolted and bounced beneath me and I felt terrible pain. Finally, the vehicle stopped and a team of medics appeared, pulling me out to see if they needed to amputate my leg in the field. Somehow, they managed to stabilize me and stop the bleeding in my leg. They attached a saline drip and shot a dose of morphine in my arm before they loaded me up again to move on.

Behind me, the carnage was real and awful. I could hear the sounds of death, the sounds of shots still being fired as our Scouts put the wounded out of their misery.

I felt physical pain and despair acutely. I wasn't prepared (nor do I believe anyone could have prepared me) to see human beings ripped apart the way I did that day. The scenes of brutal carnage kept playing over again and again in my head. I kept seeing the tearing of bodies, the explosions of people. I looked at the massive 20mm cannon sitting in the middle of the vehicle; a weapon designed to derail trains; to take out a plane that is bombing a village. It was never designed to be used on people the way it was that day.

We advanced to the next camp as planned. I was wounded and bandaged and without a weapon. We were entering another military zone and I felt completely naked without my AK-47. I had an incredible thirst; I reached down and grabbed a 2 pint bottle of water and drank it down. By some miracle, the water was cool. Throughout that day, I drank quite a lot of water and whenever I reached for the bottle it was filled and cool. It was a gift of mercy from a God I had only just met.

———

Thirty-four hours later we arrived at a remote hospital, where the doctors operated on me, saving my leg from being amputated. I was unconscious for some time but the day after the surgery I came to.

The first thing I asked about was Callie.

'Has anyone informed my wife that I'm here?'

The nurse looked at me strangely; surprised I had a family. 'No, we haven't done that, but we will.'

I imagined what it would be like for Callie; it was a wife's worst nightmare to receive a visit from the army, a uniformed officer approaching your house to deliver news of a loved one, usually dying or dead. I was sorry to send her word this way but there was no other option. (Callie still remembers the military vehicle pulling up in the front of our home and her running away from it. Her father was with her at the time and he was the one who took the message from the officer: 'Keir has been wounded, but he is alive.')

After surgery I was moved to a recovery room with a young boy who had just had his tonsils out and an Irish man who kept cracking jokes. Since I was drugged, I don't remember his Irish humor, other than that the jokes were funny and it hurt each time I laughed. The reason for the painful laughter was that I had a serious case of pneumonia in both lungs- a by-product of the morphine I had been given in the field.

Since I had narrowly escaped death, I knew that my recovery would take some time. At first I didn't respond to the antibiotic treatment they prescribed for infection. I watched doctors and nurses speaking in hushed tones around me and eventually discovered that they were considering moving me.

'What's going on?' I asked.

My doctor realized he had to tell me, but he was careful with what he said. 'There is a hospital in Salisbury that is much better equipped to deal with cases like this,' he said. 'Even so, it's a risk to move you right now.'

I nodded, agreeing. I didn't want to be moved but I knew the situation was dire. Not only was there a physical risk of moving me before I was stable enough to travel, but I was part of a covert operation –an offensive battle. Rhodesia would have a lot of explaining to do. It is one thing to defend your country against terrorism; it is quite another to forge an offensive battle against terrorists.

After some deliberation, the staff decided to take their chances and let me recover in their remote clinic. They changed the antibiotic course I was on, giving me another and hoping for the best. Their concerns were soon quieted when I responded favorably to the new antibiotics. I gained color in my face; I started eating and drinking. Soon I was able to breathe without oxygen. My leg, however, was another story.

One doctor, after examining me, confessed that he wasn't sure if I would walk again.

'If you do,' he said carefully. 'It will be with a limp. You may gain some mobility but you will always need assistance.'

'Really?' I asked him. 'We'll see about that.'

I considered his comment to be a challenge. Never walk again? Limp or need a wheelchair? I was determined to prove him wrong. Even with my cocky determination, I soon learned that recovery from this kind of injury was no picnic. My muscles and tendons had either been badly damaged or removed. I could see, just underneath my epidermis, a rearranged mass of tissue. It was a slow and painful process, but I was determined to walk and be a hundred percent when I saw Callie.

Every day, a nursing sister would take me to an area that had no obstacles and ask me to walk a few steps with her. It was excruciating at first, I could feel the pain shooting up all the way to my teeth. Day after day it was like this until I decided to turn the tables.

'Sister?' I challenged the nursing sister in charge of my recovery.

'Yes, Keir?'

'Today, why don't you get into my wheelchair so that I can push you out to the helicopter pad?'

Her face was twisted with confusion and concern. 'That is probably not a good idea.'

'Come on,' I insisted, getting to my feet and placing her in the chair. I was still bigger than she was, so she cooperated.

I held onto the handles and took my first steps. 'There, this is good,' I said. It was better this way; I was not an invalid gripping the arm of a sister for support. This way, I could push something and feel the mechanism of my leg working.

I worked out this way every day, pushing her out to the helicopter pad and back. I would return to my bed, covered in sweat but satis-fied. The doctor in charge of my recovery was shocked by my deter-mination. Each day I grew stronger; I walked further.

By the time I went home, two weeks later, I was able to stand and walk without much assistance at all.

———————

I returned home and life seemed to be fresher; I appreciated every-thing. I decided to begin a course of study to become a doctor. I had always loved the medical field and the recovery process gave me a heart for patients facing the same challenges I had. Hailing from a family of intellectuals, I was determined to make something of myself. If I had 'MB' or 'MBChB.' after my name, it would mean that I became somebody; that I had a purpose. Callie decided to go back to work in order to bring in an income. I promised her it would all be worth it and I went to universityl.

———————

One night, Callie and I went to see the movie Jesus of Nazareth. Near the beginning of the movie, the angel Gabriel visits Mary and a light shines all around her. I knew, as I watched it, that this light was ex-actly like the one that had surrounded me in battle. I knew it was the presence of God.

A few days later, we were having dinner with friends and the subject of the movie came up.

'Have you seen the movie Jesus of Nazareth?' I asked Dennis.

Dennis was my Christian friend and I knew he would confirm that the light symbolized the presence of God. Instead of answering with a textbook reply, Dennis asked me questions. He was curious about what happened to me on the battlefield and asked me to elaborate. I told him the story in detail and he listened intently.

'What an incredible thing,' he marveled. 'What did you do?'

I told him all about my confession to God and how His presence had affected me. 'I called out to him in the back of the vehicle,' I said. 'I said, 'If you want my life, Lord, you can have it!''

We were quiet for a while as I processed the weight of the experience all over again.

'Well,' Dennis asked me. 'What are you going to do now?'

'What do you mean?' I asked him.

'You said 'If you want my life, you can have it,' to God. What does that mean to you? Where will you go from here?'

I thought about it, realizing that God had truly spared my life for a purpose. I knew that God showed Himself to me in an extremely intimate way, making it possible for me to pray. 'I should pray,' I said. I knew only one way: get next to my bed and kneel down. At that very moment, I went upstairs to my bed, Dennis following me. I prayed a sincere prayer that had no formal structure or special words: 'Thank you, God. My life is yours.'

Dennis laid his hands on me afterwards. I remember feeling the Presence again as he prayed for me: 'Lord, call this man into the ministry.'

———

The following Sunday, Callie and I went to church with Dennis and his wife. It turned out that Dennis belonged to a church that was completely different from the Anglican churches I had grown up in. People were singing and clapping; I had never seen that kind of behavior in church before but I tried to sing and clap too even though it was a bit awkward. There was a woman who was standing in the row in front of me. At some point, her worship changed and she began speaking in a language that sounded Chinese. I thought it an odd thing, but as she spoke in this tongue, I felt the familiar presence of God come over me again.

The singing lasted for some time. Finally, people began sitting down so we did so as well. There was a talk called a 'sermon' so I made myself ready to listen. That morning a young man read from the Bible and began speaking about it. At one point he said something that hit me squarely between the eyes: 'It doesn't matter what you have behind your name, it's who you know that will get you into heaven.' I didn't hear much more after that. Instead, I sat and let that truth wash over me. It resonated in my head throughout the service.

At the end of his talk, the young man asked if anyone wanted to be filled with the Holy Spirit.

'Those of you who want to receive the Holy Spirit, come forward.' I felt my heart beating in me strongly, as if it was going to pop out of my chest. I went forward, Dennis following me closely.

'I want to receive the Holy Spirit,' I told the preacher. He didn't say anything but he looked to Dennis, behind me.

'It's alright, he's saved.' I had no idea what that was all about but the pastor seemed to relax.

'Alright, I'm going to pray for you,' he said. 'But I want you to close your eyes and lift your hands.'

It was my turn to be suspicious. My background as a soldier taught me never to raise my hands –admitting capture and forced surrender. I wanted to be victorious, not surrender. Close my eyes? Why?

'Let's see what God does…' the pastor said, hoping to reassure me. I looked around and realized that I would be surrendering to God, the One who knew me intimately. I decided to do what he told me to.

As he laid his hands on me, a volcano rose up inside me and I shouted, 'ABBA!'* I shouted it loudly, over and over again. I couldn't stop and I felt God moving through me. All I knew of Abba was the musical group with a lot of pop hits, but I felt this was different. It came from the deep part of my soul and the whole church broke into applause. I smile when I remember this now. I was a new believer and I didn't know why I would be applauded (which I didn't think was allowed in church) for shouting the name of a musical group. What I knew more than anything was that I was part of something much larger than the natural world that I knew; I was filled with a burning fire.

Eventually, the fire inside of me subsided, or calmed and I returned to the daylight once again. I went back to my seat, unable to explain away what had just happened.

I remember leaving that church service, people milling around me but not being concerned with what they thought of me. Instead, as I left, I looked back at the pulpit. It was a powerful place, and I was grateful for that young man who had preached and prayed for me. As I looked, I felt God speak to me: 'I'm calling you to do the same thing as he's doing.'

That day was the beginning of a new relationship. I didn't join a religion, or a club; I was changed. That day I was introduced to the One who saved me. I knew He existed, He was with me and He healed me, He was real and He was who He said He was.

---

* Gal 4:6 - *"And because you are sons, God has sent the Spirit of His Son into your hearts, crying, "Abba! Father!"*

The day I saw Saving Private Ryan in the movie theatre was many years after I had received the calling to preach the Gospel of Jesus Christ. I had been on almost every continent, preached to thousands of people, experienced and witnessed miracles.

Why would the sense memory of the Nyadzonya Raid return to me with such force? I realized that my heart, in its healing state, still had fragments of the massive ambush hiding inside it. It came to the surface that afternoon as I watched Saving Private Ryan. In many ways, I still identify with the soldier. A soldier's ever-present fear is what makes him ready to go into battle. Without it, he is a useless fool, unaware of the dangers and the obstacles to look out for. Soldiers learn to embrace this fear; they learn to live with it and fight through it.

Through the years, however, I have transitioned from a soldier to a son to a weapon. God is the commanding officer and I am not only a soldier in His army but also a weapon in His hand. In total surrender, I become useful to Him. He is able to plug me into any battle – anytime and anywhere.

I have realized that the real battles of my life will not be against a physical enemy; most of them will be fought against the present darkness of the principalities that rule this age. As we get nearer to the end times, the fighting will be more intense. Now my commanding officer is my heavenly Father; His war is won with weapons of warfare that I have learned to love and trust. Many times, they are counter to how we have been taught to fight. As we fight the spiritual enemies that all Christians must, we must do so in the way He commands us.

This is how I've learned to fight.

Keir Tayler,
16 years old

Selous Scouts'
Osprey emblem:

2

TAKING A STAND

'Therefore put on the full armor of God, so that when the day of evil comes, you may be able to stand your ground, and after you have done everything, to stand.'

Ephesians 6: NASB

My parents gave me a deep love for Rhodesia. Harry and Monica Tayler were both Scottish by heritage, but Rhodesian deep in their hearts. My paternal grandfather, Alfred Tayler, was a soldier in the First World War and was wounded, losing one of his legs. He married Emily Maud (the nurse who took care of him throughout his injury) after the war was over. They moved to Persia when it was still a British colony and there had two children: my father, Harry and my Aunt Doris (Doris Lessing, who later won the Nobel Prize for Literature).

Being adventurous, Alfred moved his family to Southern Rhodesia after accepting a concession to farm tobacco for Great Britain. They settled in Banket, 95km northwest of the capital of Salisbury (now Harare), where they promptly took up residence in a mud-hut. My father enjoyed telling me stories; painting a rustic picture of growing up. It all sounded so wonderful: my father running around the family farm positively wild, bathing in zinc baths and swimming in rivers. He learned to hunt with a rifle as a very young lad, regularly venturing out early in the morning, shooting wild game and bringing it back for his household.

My mother's upbringing was equally adventurous, she grew up in Nyasaland (now Malawi), in the shadow of Mount Mulange. My maternal grandfather Rognvald Keir Begg, was also a Scottish man. He had a great sense of adventure and moved to Nyasaland to farm the land with his wife, Mamie, and his children, my Uncle Jim and my Mum, Monica. They also lived in very humble accommodation whilst there: a brick and mud hut nestled on the side of the great mountain. (I actually visited Mum's home village many years later, where I met an ancient black man who remembered 'Bwana Begg' and took me to the house where my mother grew up, a one-roomed affair – the foundations are still there). Grandfather Rognvald died of malaria (actually of Blackwater fever, a complication of malaria where the kidneys and organs shut down) when he was relatively young, leaving my Grandmother Mamie a widow with two small children. She remarried soon afterward, and moved with her new husband and children to a more civilized environment in Rhodesia. My Mum tells me that she took to the change very well, immersing herself in school and sport. She became a champion swimmer, representing her country (Northern and Southern Rhodesia and Nyasaland) on the competitive circuit.

When my father, Harry, finished secondary school he applied to Dartmouth Naval Academy in the United Kingdom. He was accepted, making him one of only two young men chosen from Southern Rhodesia. The prestigious academy fashioned him into an officer just in time for World War II. He reported for service to the Royal Navy and served aboard two battle cruisers, the HMS Repulse and the HMS Aurora. Both ships were sunk and my father survived both shipwrecks. After the war, he returned to Rhodesia and met my mum, who had been serving in the Royal Air Force as a photographer. Almost as soon as they met, they fell in love and settled in Southern Rhodesia.

With this family history, it's no wonder I identify with pioneers.

Growing up in Southern Rhodesia, a land colonized by the British Empire, I felt very African and very British at the same time. My parents weren't strangers to the bush; they regarded it with such respect that they made sure I understood how privileged I was to live in it.

My father's employer was Ruzawi School, an Anglican preparatory boarding school for boys, where he served as the estate manager. Situated seven kilometers south of Marandellas (Marondera) in Southern Rhodesia, Ruzawi School is almost its own world with little communities orbiting it. At the center of it all was the white formal school building - a tall, white, brick structure that was famous for a massive chiming clock, towering above the second floor wall. The bells would chime every fifteen minutes, easily seen and heard by everyone nearby. Surrounding it were the dormitories, study halls, staff homes, sports fields, pools, tennis courts and the village where the indigenous people lived. Surrounding all of this was 750 acres (303.5 hectares) of Msasa woodland and a large gum tree forest.

Our own home was a cozy place, situated about 100 meters from the school, built in the traditional missionary style with a corrugated iron roof. When it rained, especially at night, the soothing sounds of drops hitting the roof relaxed me and released the fragrance of beautiful green life. The center of our home was a kitchen, complete with an anthracite stove where my mother would cook all of our meals. In the morning, I would wake to the smell of coffee and make my way to the kitchen where we would enjoy an English breakfast together. My Mum enjoyed housekeeping but also had the luxury of a domestic helper. Mum kept quite a formal garden just outside the doors, a place she absolutely loved cultivating and keeping. The school had three boreholes so we shared the blessing of an abundant water supply. Just below our house was a tennis court and in the afternoons we could hear the boys from the school playing games there, shouting out scores between volleys. Surrounding the grounds were huge rock outcroppings and the crown acacia trees that Africa is so famous for. The bird life was absolutely prolific and their chatter was alive day and night. Since we were right in the heart of the bush, it wasn't unusual to stumble upon dassies (rock rabbits) and baboons. As darkness descended, the voices of nightjars and the cries of jackals resounded all around our home.

To the north of the school was a village, a township of native Africans, called Chinyahara. Structurally, the village was divided into parts that corresponded to the massive school clock (the Village's church was at twelve o'clock, the entrance to the village was at six o'clock, the clinic was at nine o'clock and the headmen of the village stayed at three o'clock). My father was, in a manner of speaking, the liaison between the school and the villagers. Most adults living in Chinyahara worked at the school, either outside on the grounds with my father or inside with the school staff or with Sister Du Plessis, who ran the sanatorium. They held my father in high esteem, calling him Bwana Tayler.

I became known as Piccanin Bwana (the small boss). At my tender age, I believed that I was the junior liaison and that the villagers were obliged to listen to me in the same way they did my father; no one had the heart to tell me that my title was an honorary one.

As a young child, I noticed a pronounced separation between whites and blacks; there was a massive difference between the cultures. There were jobs and medical care and plenty of food for the villagers, but I could see injustice even then. My father was a man who gave respect as he got it; he never treated anyone badly that I saw. Still, I knew that workers had to respect him, not only because he was the boss, but because he was a white man and the white men always seemed to have the final say in everything. While the swimming pool, tennis courts and playing fields were maintained by the workers, they were forbidden to use these facilities recreationally. The blacks were our servants, they had less money than we did and they often lived in homes that were falling apart. We were not wealthy but I noticed that our home was significantly nicer and that we always had better things. I assumed this was because my Dad was the boss; I made no other assumptions. Our separation was not called apartheid, but I recognized that I lived in a racist society.

It never settled in my heart as fair and I marveled at the way people around me accepted the status quo. However, there were genuine friendships between the cultures, with no apparent hidden agendas. Everyone around me appeared to be happy, the school gave us a common purpose and together we focused on making things work.

Because of the security of being my father's son, my world seemed both wild and inviting on all sides, providing an ideal environment for adventure. After breakfast, Dad would dutifully go off to look after the school grounds, whistling loudly and happily. He loved life and I would eagerly shadow him, his 'normal' tasks seemed like great expeditions. I could tell he didn't mind me tagging along; he genuinely enjoyed my company. He taught me so many things, from operating a tractor and other farm machinery to camping and an appreciation of wildlife. The forest that surrounded us was our world; it held such wonderful times and the company of my father provided an unspoken example of how I was to live as a man. In addition to the grounds, there was a seemingly endless supply of bush further out, a place my father took me to and showed me how to use a rifle to hunt birds and game. I learned to hunt with him and the dogs; we'd shoot a bird, make a fire and eat the bird.

Once, on a trip into the bush, my father pointed at a herd of buffalo. 'Which one is the lead bull?' he asked. 'Show me the one who is leader of this herd' I watched him for the answer but he offered no clues. I looked over the herd and chose the largest one, hoping I was right. My father explained that I could not tell by outward appearances but should look at the way he carried himself. 'Don't be deceived by appearances,' he said. 'Watch the way he leads; watch his habits.'

He was a gentle teacher, one who carried an unusual authority. He wanted so much to pass on his love and knowledge of wildlife to me; he wanted to give me his love for nature and the preservation of it.

The values that my Dad had were deeply ingrained in me; he was strict but fair. He would have no nonsense and I deeply respected him. At night he would read the Bible aloud to me. I still remember sitting on his lap and being held in his massive arms. He genuinely loved me and took great interest in the man I would one day be-come. As a boy, he seemed larger than life to me.

My Mum was likewise influential and prominent in my early life. She was extremely feminine and tender. Having been a very successful competitive swimmer, she gave the same passion to my sister, Sue and I. Attentive and compassionate, she was a woman who felt things deeply. She had a dairy herd on our farm, naming each calf and knowing their individual personality traits. While I saw Dad as the authority in our family, I saw my Mum as the love. Even so, my sister and I knew not to confuse her gentle understanding with weakness. Mum demanded respect from everyone around her.

Growing up around Ruzawi, I had playmates who lived in Chinyahara. Gideon, Shoniwa and Garnet would accompany me on explorations and we would hunt together (although I was always the one who got to shoot the gun). On most occasions when I'd shot a bird, they would take it home for dinner to their families. When I went home with them, I was always a welcomed guest. We'd find a comfortable place outside under the trees and sit and talk after the hunt. I was able to learn their language and culture - they were eager to teach me. Their parents were polite and welcoming people; I never felt as if I was intruding when I visited.

Eventually the time came for me to start Primary School and my life changed. I was enrolled in Ruzawi as a boarder at the young age of six. Even though my home was on the school grounds, I wasn't permitted to stay there. At night I could look out of the window and see my house from the dormitory where I slept. I missed my parents desperately, especially my father, who I was used to following around. During the school day, I would sometimes see him walk by, but I knew I couldn't talk to him or even address him; school discipline was strict.

At school there were no rocks to climb, no birds to shoot. I wasn't the Piccanin Bwana who commanded respect. Instead, I was like all of the other kids, sentenced to sit still and listen to the teacher. My days were now filled with working out math's problems and learning the concepts of reading and writing; I quickly felt lost. I wasn't able to focus properly, especially with the difficult concepts of patterns and symbols. My brain would try, and then give up. I never seemed to be able to contribute anything of value in a classroom and because of this, the teachers used a word to describe me: stupid.

As if it was not bad enough to be singled out as stupid among your peers, the message was reinforced at home as well. My Mum corrected me harshly at times, warning me not to become known as the boy who dreamed away his class time and didn't take school seriously.

In the disciplined English environment of my home and school, a lot was expected of me. I knew I wasn't living up to everyone's expectations. By the time I was eight or nine years old, when the teachers would insult me I decided that I wouldn't even try. I accepted that I wasn't as smart as the other kids – in my academic family this was an epic fail. My father cruised through school (I've mentioned earlier my aunt Doris and her achievements) and my mother was also brilliant. Being stupid became, in a sense, my identity throughout my school years. I managed to do enough to advance from grade to grade but not much more.

While I barely made my way through most subjects in the classroom, I became an outstanding athlete. I excelled in almost every sport I tried. Like my Mum, I became a competitive swimmer and did quite well. At the end of a swim, I'd be hailed as the winner and congratulated with enthusiasm by both my parents; something I grew quite fond of.

I enjoyed action and found it on most playing fields, as well as in the competitive pool. I quickly realized that a certain amount of respect came with success in sport. While academics made me feel like a loser, sport made me popular and accepted. Most kids in school were able to forgive my academic shortcomings because I had such athletic success. I knew what it felt like to be ridiculed so I never did that to anyone on the sports field. While I was gifted athletically, I remained humble.

Because of this, I became a leader among my peers.

Weekends and holidays meant time at home with my family. My younger sister, Sue, and I would sit around the fireplace with our parents in our lounge and chuck on logs to build up a good blaze. My father would roast sausages on a stick over the naked flames and we would watch them sizzle and fry, the smell would permeate the room. We'd eat them right there as a family, each of us having one or two, dipping them in tomato sauce. Afterwards, we'd sit around the fire and listen to my parents' music or listen to their stories of growing up. It seems like such a simple thing but it was most delightful for all of us to be together so unhurried and relaxed in each other's company.

Coming home for holidays also meant camping with my Dad.

It was such an adventure to pack up all of our gear and hike out – I'd have my father's undivided attention and I was in heaven! Sometimes we would set up camp at a place we called Dzwetsindi, a forested area near a river not far from our home. On those trips, my sister, Sue, and our two Alsatians, Shaun and Damon, would join us. We would make a grass basher out of the surrounding vegetation and assemble mattresses from wild grasses that we would lie on at night. Even though it wasn't far, it was worlds away from the house – leopards, baboons and other wild things were always lurking in the shadows. My Mum was always a bit too English for camping, it wasn't something she enjoyed. She often said she had done enough in her life already.

'I'll join you for dinner, round the fire' she'd say. 'But I will not sleep in the bush, I've done that too often, thank you very much.' She enjoyed nature just as much as we did but even a night at Dzwetsindi was too much for her. She needed the luxury of her own bed rather than the bush accommodation the rest of us loved. Sometimes she'd spend the day with us as we enjoyed the bush, but at night she would just

disappear and I knew she'd gone home. Exploring during the day
(climbing rocks and searching out caves) and sitting around the fire,
talking and laughing was like heaven for me. We didn't have electron-
ic games or iPads, we didn't even have TV. The greatest treat in those
days was that I got to camp in the wild with Dad, my sister and the
dogs – and none of us had to bath for the three or four days we were
away.

Before you think my life at home was easy, I must share a memory
that will illustrate the strict upbringing I lived with. One morning
when I was about eight or nine years old, I remember our family had
just sat down to breakfast at the kitchen table. Before I could make
myself comfortable, my father asked me a favor.

'Keir, before you sit down will you please go to my wardrobe and get
me one of my handkerchiefs?'

I said yes and went to his room, looked on the top of his wardrobe
where he normally kept them, and found none. I returned to the
table empty handed, which surprized him.

'They're not there,' I said simply as I sat down. I was ready to tuck into
breakfast when my father spoke up again.

'Son, they're there. Go and stand up on your toes and look carefully.
They will be there if you look carefully.'

I stood up and went to go and look again. I did what he asked; I
stood on my toes and looked carefully but there were no handkerchiefs there. I knew exactly where they were supposed to be, but
there were absolutely none there. When I returned I was determined
to get my point across.

'Dad, you bloody fool, there are no handkerchiefs there.'

The mood in the room changed completely . It was as if the air froze
and time stood still. My Mum looked at me, shocked; my sister almost
dropped her glass of milk.

'Keir,' my father said quietly and steadily. 'Go to your room.'

Oh… did I know I was in trouble. I suddenly realized what words had
come out of my mouth and I marched to my room, knowing the Third
World War was about to start. Filled with fear, I sat on the edge of
the bed and saw my father stand up calmly, walk outside and go to a

peach tree and extract a branch from it with his pocketknife. He knew I could see him and he made deliberate steps to skim each twig from it and did a few practice strokes in the air with it. From where I sat, it looked scary. Staying in my line of sight, he marched back into the house and calmly walked down the hall and into my room.

'Do you know why you're going to get a hiding, my boy?' he asked me, still calm.

'I do, Dad,' I replied, near tears. 'I'm sorry; I shouldn't have said that to you.'

I wondered if he could see how terrified I was; I was trembling as I lay down on my bed. My backside exposed, my father mercilessly delivered six strong strokes as I screamed my objections. I stood up afterwards, tears streaming down my face; I couldn't sit down but walked around my room, crying. My sister, Sue, was crying her eyes out in the hallway. Mum was furious with Dad, thinking he had gone too far. I could hear her being upset with him back in the kitchen. I was in pain and each welt was rising up and stinging terribly but at the same time, I knew Dad was right to give me a hiding. I knew I deserved correction.

Finally, my father came back to my room. He sat down in a chair and brought me in front of him. He looked straight at me and I could see his gentleness again.

'Son, I had to give you a hiding. I had to teach you a lesson.'

'I know Dad, I know.'

'You just can't speak to me like that.'

'I know, Dad, I'm sorry.'

He looked at me; and I could no longer stay away from him. I went to him and he scooped me up in his big arms and sat me down on his lap. I cried and cried against his chest, mostly because of the physical pain. I had nowhere else to go for comfort but to him, even though he was responsible for the pain I was feeling.

Days later, once I was back at school, I showed off my welts to my friends.

'Hey, check this,' I said, showing them my welts like they were battle scars.

'What happened?' They were shocked - all of my friends asked how I got them.

'My Dad gave me a hiding,' I said. I proceeded to tell them the story, leaving nothing out. In those days, we'd exchange stories of parental discipline like soldiers traded war stories.

'Wow,' they said, once I'd finished. 'That's pretty bad.'

'Yeah,' I agreed. 'It was rough. But I deserved it.'

As we spread out on the playground, one of my friends said something I'll never forget. He said it in a way that made me feel sad for him.

'I wish my dad would do that with me,' he said.

'Why?' I asked.

'I wish I knew where my boundaries were.'

I realized, then, that my welts were stripes of a prize. I had the prize of a father who loved me enough to show me I couldn't cross the boundary line without suffering a consequence.

———

Marandellas High School was a new school, situated in a small town not far from the country setting I was raised in. I enrolled there when it was time and soon found that a lot of incompetent teachers worked there, ones who would devalue the students. One of the history teachers I had (when I didn't pass an exam) would assign screeds and screeds of chapters I would have to copy and write as a punishment for not focusing. Know what it taught me? To hate him even more.

Each week my father and mother would write letters to me. I enjoyed getting the letters and realized that our relationship was maturing. Their letters were more than a report of what was going on at home; they were heartfelt instruction from parents who were trying to pass on wisdom. I read them and reread them to encourage me while I was away from them.

Secondary school is usually the time in a young man's life that shapes who he is, that exposes what is really important in his heart and what is still being negotiated. I was quickly singled out for leadership by the administration and given responsibility for leading my fellow students. This would color the way I led for the rest of my life.

Marandellas School had the traditional academic programme seen in most schools in Rhodesia at the time. It had living quarters, or hostels, that housed otherwise wild young men and encouraged them to become studious. I was appointed head prefect of my hostel, the leader who was expected to set a standard among the other prefects and fellow students who stayed there. As unsavory as it sounds, I loved the job as prefect. I found it suited my desire for justice and honed my ability to enforce it. It also made me realize that some of my peers didn't have as strong a sense of right and wrong as I did.

My fellow prefects and I saw ourselves differently - the prefects in our hostel decided that they wanted their own rooms. They approached our headmaster and asked for this privilege as a perk of the job we held. The headmaster considered it but in the end respectfully denied the request.

I understood and accepted his controversial decision but many of my fellow prefects resigned. Since I remained a prefect and acquiesced, I became very unpopular with the rest of the boys and actually lost a lot of my credibility. My ability to enforce the rules among my peers at the hostel suffered as a consequence.

During this time, a senior boy who we called Cabbage (a nickname given to him because of his hair – a large frizzy helmet that resembled a cabbage) decided to make me look foolish among my fellow residents. He had a reputation for being aggressive, manipulative and a bit of a bully. He pushed the boundaries daily and manipulated his friends into the same rebellion that he practiced.

One evening, everything blew up. It was a night like any other; the students were working on their homework in their cubicles in our study hall. Cabbage wasn't fond of homework and usually caused distractions during this time. I heard him talking loudly to his fellow seniors and I got up from my table and walked over to his cubicle.

'Cabbage, you know the rules. It's time to be quiet and do your homework.'

'Oh, yes,' he said. 'Sorry.'

I went back to my table and sat back down, only to hear the same chattering going on a few minutes later. This time I didn't give him the courtesy of correcting him in private. I stood up and lifted my voice so that all the students could hear.

'Cabbage,' I said, looking squarely at him. 'I have asked you to keep quiet already tonight. Now, I'm telling you to shut up and sit down. We all have work to do.'

You could have cut the tension in the air with a chainsaw. There was an unspoken rule that prefects could not openly correct the senior boys. I had everybody's attention and people looked over at him to see how he'd react. Cabbage gave a slow smile. He was the reigning ringleader of the hostel; I was the turncoat prefect.

He stood up, leaned over his cubicle and returned my stare. 'Make me.'

'Alright,' I said, putting down my pen. 'You had better come outside with me right now.'

A hush swept through the room and I walked out to the square piece of lawn just outside the hall. I could feel others following me, including Cabbage. It was half-light and the evening had not yet brought the privacy of darkness.

I turned around and faced off with Cabbage, who was pretty big. The thought of winning or losing the fight had not crossed my mind; I only knew that words had no power over him.

'I am in charge here, Cabbage,' I said. 'My job as a prefect is to keep everybody quiet during homework time and if anyone makes a noise I'll shut him up. You got that?'

'Really?' he was smiling; I knew he thought he could take me.

'Since you don't respect the authority of my words, I have to challenge you. I warned you to shut up and you haven't…'

'You are a fool,' Cabbage said, suddenly. 'I'll prove to you right now that you can't tell me what to do.'

Before he could say anything else, I threw a punch to his face. The fight was on, and it was knuckles and hits; throwing punches and painful jabs. In the next few minutes I think I received more than I gave: possibly thirty hits or so to my face and chest.

Cabbage started holding back; I think he could see he was inflicting too much damage. Blood was everywhere. 'Why don't you give up?' he said, breathlessly. 'I'm only going to hurt you more.'

'I will never quit,' I said, spitting blood as I spoke. Tears were streaming down my face. 'Even if I don't hit you, I will never quit!' I still had hold of his shirt and I wouldn't give up. 'My job might seem silly to you, but I'm going to do it, you got it?' He stepped back and I could see in his eyes that he regarded me differently. The other students watched in dumbfounded amazement.

The fight had taken a lot out of us but Cabbage and I stood there, both of us breathless and unbending. I knew that he finally saw clearly who I was; more importantly, so did the other students.

'If you talk again,' I panted. 'I'm going to correct you. If you don't listen to me, I will bring you outside and fight you again. I am not afraid of you.'

He didn't say anything, but as I moved to go inside, he stepped aside. I went to the bathroom to wash my face. The rest of the students, including Cabbage, went back into the hall.

I washed my face in the bathroom and saw how badly I had been beaten. Cabbage had given better blows than I had but it didn't make him the victor. I stubbornly washed, despite the pain. When I went back into the hall, everyone was looking at me.

I stood up as straight as I could, boldly making an announcement to everyone.

'I fought Cabbage because he refused to listen to what I said. I may not have hit as well as he did, but if anyone violates the principles of this hostel I will take you outside and give you some of the same. I will not quit, I am a prefect, and you will listen to what I say. Is that clear?'

The boys looked back at me, then nodded. I waited a few seconds and then sat down; no one said a thing.

After that night I never had trouble with any of them, especially Cabbage.

While we were fairly insulated in Rhodesia, none of us could escape the news of rising tension in the country. Whilst in High School, I learned that Ian Smith had declared independence from Great Britain, since the British were ready to walk away from Rhodesia and hand it over to unsteady and dangerous leadership.

There were two main groups opposing white minority rule: the ZANU-PF (Zimbabwe African National Union – Political Front) and

ZIPRA (ZImbabwe People's Revolutionary Army). Their leadership was a collection of men with military backgrounds but they couldn't seem to agree with the other party long enough to unite against the demon of 'white minority rule'. In building up their own armies to fight 'Ian Smith and the Nationals' both groups decided to resort to terrorist activities and guerilla warfare. Robert Mugabe, the leader of the ZANU-PF decided to strike the hardest. He demanded a new land with black leadership, but he also seemed to be a power-hungry man who fought just as fiercely against the ZIPRA black leadership. News reached us of unexpected attacks and of village youths being kidnapped to be used as soldiers. He seemed wild and unstoppable; wanting control and using any means necessary to get it. It was terrorism, pure and simple. Our country was on the brink of allout civil war.

———

During this unstable time, I was scheduled to take my O level exams (the ordinary exams that all students needed to pass secondary school). I tried to study, but I knew it was no use. The subjects I had barely passed during my high school career would now be examined and I would be expected to remember everything at once. I knew I would fail before I even sat for my exams. The day the results were delivered, my mother read the ominous verdict: I had failed. I was, after all this time, still stupid. She shook her head in disgust.

'Well, you failed. You're the one who is going to tell your father.'

I trudged out to him; he was busy in the forest, the wild place where we used to spend so much time together. He looked up as I approached him and as soon as he saw me, he knew I brought news of my exams. He further knew from my countenance that I had failed; I didn't even need to say anything.

'When are you going to learn to grow up and be responsible?' he asked me, angrily. I could tell he was genuinely concerned about what would happen to me. 'Everyone has to finish secondary school! Your life is passing before you; the future is not so far away! It's right here!' My father was a successful man who was militant in his actions and thought; I knew from his stance that failure wasn't an option but what could I do? I didn't know how to write an exam and pass.

After some careful assessment and deliberation, my father decided that I would enlist in the army. Since Rhodesia was about to head into a terrible civil war, fighting terrorists like Mugabe, troops were needed and they didn't care if I was brilliant at maths or a failure at English. I was suddenly excited about the prospect of being a soldier; glad that I didn't have to wrestle with the idea of school anymore.

'Don't think it's over,' my father warned me. 'You'll finish these courses at home, through a correspondence school.'

Over the next three months, while I waited to go into the army, I studied at my bedroom table – Tayler College. It was an important time: I could finally be successful or a failure forever; it was up to me.

I set about planning each day. I disciplined myself with a mixture of physical fitness, study and self-imposed rewards. I loved it.

My parents didn't interfere; only encouraged me to continue. I got into a routine of study, without the distraction of sport or being a prefect. I buckled down and did it.

I finished.

———

A few months after I mailed in my exams, I received my call-up papers to report to Llewellyn Barracks. My parents dropped me off at the train station, where they wished me well and watched me board my train with nothing more than a small suitcase of essential belongings. I was officially headed off into the army, enlisted in a program they had for 'school leavers.' On the train, I met others guys like me; all bound for boot camp that would force us to become men quickly. On the ride over, we exchanged 'war stories' of what we had heard about Llewellyn's staff; they were reportedly monsters, feeding on young men like us. We knew it was going to be brutal; all of us would be thrown into quite a different life. The disciplined environments of the boarding schools we came from would look like a holiday camp.

As soon as we arrived at the station, we saw them, two stone-faced corporals waiting for the train to come to a complete stop. As soon as it did, they started screaming at the top of their lungs for us to fall into order; line up and shut up. We did so to the best of our ability but, of course, we could do nothing right and they shouted insults in our faces just to show us that they were in command. It was a cold morning and we had to stand perfectly still at attention for quite some time. When they had decided that we were sufficiently whipped, we were loaded into the backs of trucks – 15 to 20 men to each truck - and taken to Llewellyn Barracks. We stopped outside a massive hangar, where we had to line up in alphabetical order and perfectly straight. One by one we were lined up, shorn and shoved into line again. A basic military kit that contained the only clothes I would wear for the next few months was shoved into my hands. As we exited the other side, another corporal was waiting for us, holding a Bible out for us to swear on. We had to lay our hands on it and swear allegiance to Rhodesia; to swear to defend her with honor. I was no longer Keir Tayler; I was now a number and a rank, property of the Rhodesian Army.

We filed into barracks and were told where to sleep, how to do our bedroll. All the while, the NCO's were shouting at us as if we were dirt. The sergeant knew us all to be worthless beings, barely worth keeping alive in the hope that one day we would become soldiers. Even though I knew that discipline and order were necessary, it was still rough getting used to it. As rough as my father was, as serious a disciplinarian, he was not like the army. As rigid and uncompromising as my colonial boarding school was, the staff was there for me – I was one of them. I wasn't accustomed to being esteemed as nothing; being yelled at constantly.

The army woke me up: I was now on my own and whether or not I survived and stood out would depend on how I obeyed. I was deter-mined to become a trustworthy soldier.

One day a sergeant approached me, carrying a big envelope.

'Here,' he said, handing it to me. 'I believe this is for you.' After thank-ing him in proper military fashion, I looked down at it. It was the results of my written correspondence exams. With my hands shaking, I opened it to see the verdict. What I saw shocked me. Not only had I passed, I had graduated with honors.

Many times we can believe wrong things about ourselves. We can hear messages as children that become deeply ingrained in us; messages that may not be true. Once I started reading and memo-rizing passages of the Bible, I realized that God, the author of truth, said different things about me. I not only chose to believe this truth; I began speaking it over myself. It is now the reason I can stand tall.

Often when people hear the term 'Father God' they have a picture in their mind, which is a distorted view of what a father should be.

This destroys their ability to relate to God as the perfect Heavenly Father. Many people don't have a good role model of what a father is here on earth. They might have had a father who has let them down (adultery, divorce, etc.) So they haven't had a clear picture of what a real father is supposed to look and act like.

Many times I have used the term 'Father God' to people and I see an instant barrier or wall that goes up. I can tell they've never experienced a father as loving, merciful and gracious. A father is supposed to be on your side; the one who has fought for you, cheered for you, encouraged you.

They sometimes say things to me, like: 'You mean God is a father? My father was a big jerk; he was never really there for me. My father was abusive; my father was unfair. He degraded me; I couldn't trust him.'

We live in a world with dysfunctional families. My own wasn't perfect, but when I heard the term 'Father God' I was able to take the best things I remembered about my earthly father and apply them to my heavenly Father.

Since our views of God and heaven are sometimes based on earthly models, the church has to bring an understanding of the Father where one has never been. Sometimes even when the church has an opportunity to be a father to young men and women who have had a distorted model of a father, they can get it wrong.

Unconditional love is our only hope. Every kid fights for acceptance, love and attention. Sometimes kids will even turn your face towards them to receive that eyeball-to-eyeball contact: undivided attention. We are given that from our Heavenly Father, unconditional love. We find the definition of truth in the Bible. In its pages, we see a God who is real take shape and come to life. One who is as fair as He is perfect; One who has the same standards and heart for everyone, regardless of status or brains or strength.

Getting my value from the Word of God was the thing that changed my life. I realized that I wasn't stupid; I had everything I needed with God. He was the One who gave me His Word to heal me. He sent His only Son to save me; that's what He thinks of me.

As much as it seems simple, the weapon of the Word of God is the only true thing with the power to transform and to bring restoration. It makes those of us who have weak legs stand among those giants

Keir and his mother,
Monica Tayler

Keir and his sister,
Sue as kids

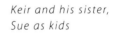
Sergeant Major K. Tayler,
Selous Scouts

Keir Tayler on Ops, Rhodesia

Keir walking through a mine field at
Mukumbura to a meeting

Pioneering on
'roads' in Africa

Training church
leaders

Keir, Mum, Dad,
Peggy (Callie's
Mum holding
Simon), Ian (Callie's
Dad), Callie, Rory,
Jane and Jenni
(bottom right).
Rory and Jane
married - Jane is
Callies twin sister.

Kashel Mlotwa

The Tayler family, 1980

Tea with pastors, planning an event, in remote Africa.

Keir & Callie in the 1990's

Beautiful moments in a travelling life

Outdoor power evangelism meeting - Simon sitting next to the Pastor.

Street meeting: healing and Evangelism in Namibia.

we were once afraid of. It transforms us from frightened children who feel stupid into soldiers equipped to carry His message into the world.

It comes back to this: Do you believe in God the Father? Do you believe in His one and only Son Jesus Christ? If so, it will be all you need to transform you into the soldier you need to be in the end times.

In the next chapter, I will tell you how truth and righteousness changed my life; you won't believe where I found it. They are the weapons of warfare that we can put on every day, ones that equip us to discern the truth from all of the lies in this world.

Rifleman Tayler (near top and center), Llewellyn Barracks

RIGHTEOUS TRUTH

'Stand firm then, with the belt of truth buckled around your waist, with the breastplate of righteousness in place,'

Ephesians 6:14 NASB

Swimming can be a lonely sport. One competitor swims against five to seven others and performance is dependent upon the preparation put in beforehand. The moment you dive into the water, the world becomes silent and the only sounds you hear are your breathing, the water and your heartbeat echoing in your ears. Once you pour everything into swimming against the inertia of the water, there is a sense of rhythm as you 'eat up' the meters before you. I grew accustomed to putting into each race what I wanted to get out.

Growing up as a competitive, purposeful swimmer (as my Mum was before me) I knew the disciplines of goal setting; I was familiar with the training required to succeed. I knew how to rise above pain and fatigue to accomplish a goal.

I found that the same principles applied in the Army; I took to it as the proverbial fish takes to water.

Llewellyn Barracks was my new home; guys in battalions were forced to live together, side-by-side. The sergeant in charge of us imposed basic disciplines, many of which seemed surprising and new to my roommates. In the battalions we all had authority imposed upon us. We were forced, as a group of men to listen to the voice of one man commanding us; and then to obey as one man. When we heard a command, we executed it absolutely; knowing that in combat there would be no time for questions. To our commanding officers, we were the lowest of the low, spoken to as if we were absolute dirt.

To ourselves, we were all different people coming from different parts of the country. We had to form some kind of friendship with this terror roaring down on us. We got to know each other pretty well and I started realizing that a lot of these guys weren't like me at all; many of the men lacked discipline. My sergeant singled me out as a leader because I did things exactly as I was told – sometimes even before I was told. While I was expected to motivate my fellow soldiers, I felt that I was surrounded by fellows who didn't take their duties seriously. Many of them wanted to take short cuts. There was a collective conscience to never volunteer for anything. When someone escaped duty regularly, he was revered as a hero. I had seen this at school and had hated it thentoo. Pandering to peer-pressure was a weakness, in my eyes. Peer-pressure was herd mentality and I called this behavior 'remaining beige' ('beige' meant average and pathetic, mundane and nondescript, just as the color is.) I was determined to live my life in a scarlet hue, full of opportunity, to be alive out loud.

After doing our basic training we had one month 'call-outs' (where we had to spend a month in the bush defending our nation against Communist intruders). On one of the monthly "call-outs", I was told to go out with a detail to set up what was called S Tank – a portable swimming pool used for washing and cleaning up. We were on the northeast corner of the country, right on the border of Zambia, in a real bush situation and there were no rivers or lakes around. I went out with my troop to set up this S tank and we chose a location underneath the shade of a tree in a sandy place suitable for the bottom of the tank. It was considered to be a red area (hot for terrorists), so some of us dug while the others kept watch for snipers. While I was surveying the area a shot rang out and a bullet suddenly hit the sand right in front of me. When the bullet made impact, sand shot up in my face, startling me terribly. I ran to the Land Rover and got my rifle, raising it and releasing automatic fire into the reeds while the men took cover. In the riverbed we were virtually sitting ducks, so I scanned the horizon for the sniper. Suddenly, out of nowhere, three men appeared, walking towards me and I heard the voice of our Lieutenant on my radio, saying that he was approaching us. My finger was on the trigger and I was mid-squeeze when I realized that the 'sniper' was my own lieutenant, a man I could have dropped if I had shot, which I would have had cause to do. Finally he came up to us, smiling and flippant.

'Did I wake you boys up?' he asked me.

'What the 8#$* did you think you were doing?' I shouted. 'I could have dropped you!' Then, just to keep with military tradition, I added: 'Sir.'

'I didn't think you would be so aggressive Corporal,' he said.

'I didn't think you would be such a fool to test us … Sir.'

The man was a joker who didn't hold the lives of others in any kind of esteem, to say nothing of his own life. He was an officer, but his 'caliber' proved him to be someone who was an extremely hard soldier to follow into battle. Nevertheless, he was a lieutenant- I was merely a soldier. Who was I to correct him?

Behavior like this made me less and less desirous of staying in the battalions and more and more desirous of moving on to the Special Forces.

The Special Forces were made up entirely of volunteers; all had to be self-disciplined and self-motivated. They were serious soldiers, each one exuding courage, honor and dignity. Once enrolled, they pursued specialized disciplines: parachuting, aqua, sharpshooting, tracking, survival and demolitions. They were required to be ultra-fit, skilled with machinery and weaponry of all kinds. They seemed ready for anything and I wanted to be one of them.

Almost as soon as I could, I volunteered. There was a kindred spirit among the Special Forces -a good, solid camaraderie right away. We were no longer pipsqueak rookies; still unknown or tested in battle but once we were trained, we could inflict serious damage if we were allowed to.

Suddenly, there were no requirements like marching or keeping your bedroll a certain way. Instead, I realized that discipline would be self-imposed; there were different expectations and added responsibilities. In my new assignment, I was aware that I was face to face with more serious consequences. In the Battalions, if you're caught sleeping on duty, you would be disciplined; in Special Forces if you were caught sleeping on duty you were Court-martialed and automatically expelled.

In its embryonic stages, the Selous Scouts were called 'Tracker Combat Unit': thirty-two of us who knew how to track. This small group then went through a selection course and specific training to become the nucleus of Selous Scouts Territorial Force (civilians who volunteered to become soldiers). The Scouts were an elite group that selected the best from both Battalions and Special Forces and then tested them physically and emotionally to levels beyond what humans should be able to bear.

It was unique training. Apart from the extreme physical challenges (like forced food deprivation and sleeplessness) there were psychological tests of strength.

Many professional soldiers came to us from the Rhodesian Light Infantry and the elite SAS. They would volunteer for the Selous Scouts, thinking they'd be moved to the front of the queue. In reality, the toughest test for them was to go through the same training we all had to go through at the beginning. There was no differentiation or favoritism - Our motto was 'pamwe chete' - which in the Shona language means 'all together' good and bad. We had no hierarchy or racism – anyone could shoot or stop a bullet.

On the second day, all the recruits would be taken to the rifle range to have their weapons zeroed. They would have to sit through a lecture on how to set up a base-camp in the bush. Some of the 'professionals' that came to us would absolutely lose their cool.

'What do you think I am?' One of them screamed in the instructor's face. 'I am not a recruit! I am a soldier with five years of action and you want me to zero my weapon and teach me basics? We are Special Forces and you treat us as rookies! This is an insult! I didn't come here for this!'

The instructor would secretly be hoping for this kind of insubordination. It would weed out the selfish ones right away. It would also be fun to correct

'Soldier, come here! What did you say? Did I hear you murmuring and whinging about this Unit?'

The recruit would seldom think twice about his outburst. 'Yes Sir!'

'Do you see that kraal over there?' The isntructor would point to a structure we had erected for show-offs who did not make the grade – a holding pen for failures.

'Yes Sir' the recruit said, a little less enthusiastically.

'Get your gear and stay there until further orders – Is that clear? You have failed. Dismissed!'

We had no use for unteachable, arrogant professionals with selfish attitudes. We called them 'medal hunters' – the guys who would have total disregard for fellow soldiers while they were playing the heroes. In the dangerous fields of war this was a weakness – it could be exposed in proper training, if we were careful.

Insubordination, speaking against an instructor and lowering team morale were the most common reasons that professional soldiers failed the Scouts. Lack of discipline and general bad attitude were easy to sort out among soldiers - we pushed them until they chose to quit. The course was designed to push a man to his absolute limit in seventeen days. If you volunteered and survived the selection process, you were given a belt and beret that you could wear with pride. The Scout uniform commanded instant respect.

Those who were not selected were not seen as failures. They could look someone in the eye and hold their heads up, knowing they had tried. No sensible man would ever accuse them of failing, there was no such thing. Many who were not selected rose up in the ranks as soon as they returned to the barracks, their dignity intact. Volunteering and not being selected was seen as a gutsy move but I survived the training process and became belted and bereted. It was my new identity: I was a Selous Scout. I stood tall among the best of the best.

———·

After completing the selection course for the Selous Scouts, I was enrolled to be part of an upcoming advanced tracking course before I could be deemed fully operational. I trained with weights at a gymnasium 'eight days a week', for the sheer joy of it with my friend, John Bragge. In those days we could both bench press 300 pounds and love it. One afternoon John told me that he had been invited to a very swanky wedding to be held at the Ambassador Hotel; the wedding was the next day and he hadn't found a date.

'Look at the invitation,' he showed me. 'It says it is for me and a partner. You're my gym partner. Want to go with me? There's bound to be plenty of girls there.'

As a red-blooded male, girls were always the subject of discussion but I knew there would be no sense in beginning a new relationship. In a few weeks I would be off to the bush war and who knew what would happen? Nevertheless, I took John up on his invitation. What John failed to tell me was that the wedding was actually for the

Deputy Prime Minister's daughter, so there would be quite a bit of security surrounding it. John and I sauntered into the hotel and headed towards the reception area just in time for the Master of Ceremonies to make his speech. We appeared in the doorway and the place fell silent. We looked more like hired thugs than wedding guests and someone in charge soon approached us, asking if he could help.

'Yes, we're invited to this wedding,' John removed the invitation from his jacket pocket.

'Really?' The guy looked at us suspiciously. 'It says here Mr John Bragge and partner...'

'Yeah, this guy is my gym partner. I don't have a girl partner today, unfortunately.'

After some deliberation, the man allowed us to stay (I think he was a little afraid of us). We quickly found the two nearest available seats and ordered drinks. Across the table from me was a stunning young woman and her friend – young ladies who sized us up and quickly went off to the bathroom. John and I looked at each other. Had we scared them off? Embarrassed them? We were there as wedding guests but it was easy for people to tell that we weren't really acquainted with either the bride or the groom. We tried to play it cool, but we were still gentlemen beneath our rough exteriors. We knew that it was awkward to show up late for a wedding and then sit across from two young ladies and scare them off.

Thankfully, the young ladies returned. The pretty one introduced herself to me as Callie. John and I were relieved and grateful that she took pity on us. She was all grace and ease and soon made us feel as if we belonged at the table. Callie was both a gifted conversationalist and a good listener. And she looked at me as I spoke. It was hard for me to ignore that she was classically beautiful as I tried to pay attention to the conversation. I was totally attracted to her; she had incredible blue eyes set against creamy white skin and jet-black hair. She seemed to command respect and I was absolutely enthralled. As the evening proceeded, John and I suggested that we all leave the wedding and head off to another place that could be more fun. Callie accepted, her eyes sparkling in anticipation.

There was a nightclub nearby with dancing and music, we decided to go there. When we arrived, I realized that I had no money to get into the club, so I had no choice but to leave. I wanted to offer to escort

Callie home but my only means of transport was a motorcycle. As Callie was in a dress; I couldn't take her anywhere. As soon as I made sure that she was taken care of and had a ride home; I apologized for the unfortunate series of events. She seemed fine and thanked me for a wonderful evening. It was terrible and I was embarrassed. I liked her but I knew that I was in no position to offer her anything, not even a ride. I was headed into the Scouts and I didn't have time for a serious relationship.

I entered (and completed) the Advanced Tracking Course, which turned out to be as vigorous as it sounded. Now I was ready to be released into duty and I was excited at the prospect.

In the meantime, I still worked at the veterinary lab bringing in an income. It was a decent place to work and I enjoyed the company of my co-workers. We all loved sport and decided to form a workplace hockey team and join a league where we would compete against other commercial teams. One day, during hockey season (a couple of months after the wedding) we played a game on the field at the George Hotel. Afterwards, as I was reclining in a chair having a coke, who should walk by but the fabulously beautiful Callie! I jumped to my feet and skidded over to her, stopping in front of her and greeting her. She greeted me, collected and coy.

'You do look familiar, I think I've met you before, haven't I?' She tells me now that her heart was racing and she knew exactly who I was.

I found out that she was going to a Ladies' Night at the neighboring nightclub. She was with friends and they were meeting for a few hours to socialize undisturbed. I asked Callie if she would mind if I joined her after the Ladies' time. I told her that since I stayed relative-ly far away, I would rock up wearing hockey shorts and with stock-inged feet (I promised I would remove my boots with the studs). She agreed and I did just that – Callie wasn't embarrassed at all. We talked and danced all night and had a great time together.

After this night, we decided to see each other regularly. I took her to the movies (not really a productive date – we were both looking at the screen and not talking). I invited her to come along on a camping trip I was planning to take with my sister and her friends. A whole crowd of us went and I was in my element. We had no tents, only sleeping bags and essentials. I was in charge of the cooking and I decided to impress her with my favorite dinner: Coke, Sadza (the

Rhodesian traditional maize-meal staple) and sausages roasted over a naked flame. Callie was not impressed at all; she told me so, laughing.

That night, under a starry sky, Callie and I lay on our sleeping bags by the fire, chucking logs on it to keep us warm. I realized, as we talked, that we actually had quite a bit in common. We talked all night and eventually I went to sleep, thinking about how wonderful she was.

We saw each other quite often and grew closer as friends. She had been raised just like me, so she had learned how to buffer loneliness and tragedy with a great sense of humor. She understood how to be a powerful and yet gentle woman; she inspired me to be a better man. She had integrity and character that was visible in both the small and large decisions she made in her life. Almost instantly I realized I could trust her.

The time came for me to meet her parents, Ian and Peggy. It turned out that they had similar histories to my own parents, adventurers who wanted a better life. They came to Africa from Great Britain, settling in Rhodesia. They had pilgrim spirits like my own family and I was very comfortable around them.

After meeting her family, I knew the next step was for her to meet mine. Callie felt the very thing with my parents as I had with hers. We felt at home in each other's families; it was miraculous. The first afternoon with them, my father invited me to come out with him on a private walk around the farm, like old times. I was so comfortable to be back in that place with my Dad. I wasn't expecting him to ask what he did.

'What are your intentions with this woman?'

I thought about Callie, especially how she communicated to me about her dreams and hopes for life. It took a moment to translate what I felt for her deep in my heart. I struggled for the words, but I finally said what I knew for sure. 'I really like this girl; she seems special and different.'

He turned around and looked at me in the eye. 'You'd be a fool if you didn't marry this girl.'

I realized he was right; I wanted to marry her. After he said this aloud, it was like my thoughts and desires became clear. Callie was more than my girlfriend; she was my future wife. As soon as I realized this, I asked her to marry me. I didn't need much time to think about it; I was sure that she would be the woman I wanted to come home to forever. She would be the mother of my children; she would be the one I would share my life with.

We were married within five months. I fought for her, knowing that she was a woman who many men would be trying to marry. Being competitive, I was determined to win her over all of her other suitors. In Callie's mind, it was done that first day. That terrible evening at the wedding where I was so awkward and disjointed was the day that Callie decided in her heart that I was her husband. She tells the story now of coming home to her mother and telling her: 'Guess what? Today I met the man I'm going to marry!'

Callie and I were wed on 21 December 1974. It was a very happy time and I felt the joy of knowing that she was my wife. Jenni was born two years later and my life was one explosion of happiness. Everything became so real and so tender; there was now so much I had to protect. In those days I had three things that occupied my time: work at the vet lab, the army and my time with Callie. I knew that as a volunteer Selous Scout I could be called into a bush war at any moment.

———

This brings us to where my story began- Operation Eland (the Nyadzonya Raid). My introduction to the reality of war was horrific and proved to have long lasting consequences.

During my time of recovery I was sidelined by the army, giving me ample time to recover. It was a time of reflection as well as healing and (as I said previously) I realized that I had always been drawn towards the medical field. Now that I was face to face with doctors who were involved in bringing me to a place of health and restoration, I realized that I wanted to do the same: help broken people be restored to health and be part of their transformation.

After talking to Callie about it, I decided that I would begin studying medicine. Since I was twenty-seven years old, I wasn't sure if the medical school would even accept my application. It turned out the school knew who I was and my history in the Selous Scouts, and gladly granted me admission. This surprising news threw us into frenzied planning to see how we could make this new direction possible. We decided that the best course of action would be for Callie to go back to work to pay for tuition and books; Jenni, our young daughter was put into crèche at a very tender age.

———

The day of my true salvation (the day in church when I shouted 'ABBA!' over and over again) I walked to the back of the church and turned around to look back at the altar. There was a weighty sense of a spiritual presence, as if God Himself was speaking, saying, 'Son, I've called you to do the same thing that that preacher was doing.'

I grew very emotional and I couldn't speak. When Callie or Dennis asked me what was happening, I couldn't explain –every time I tried to explain, I would burst into tears. We all had lunch afterward and life carried on; no one seemed too worried that I wasn't joining in the conversation. Dennis looked at me and smiled, saying, 'It's alright, Keir. Everyone can tell that God has His hand on you.'

I didn't know what he meant; the experience was very foreign and I was unprepared for it. I kept thinking about that lady in front of me who had been speaking Chinese. How did someone like that affect me so much? Why did this 'ABBA!' come out of my mouth so quickly, over and over?

Later that night, after Callie had gone off to bed, I sat down outside our cottage and looked up at the stars.

'Lord, if you want to come now, then come.' His presence was so tangible; I thought God might just appear physically before me. I had no idea how He usually did things, other than the miracles I read about in the Bible. I had no cause to doubt that He could appear physically. He didn't appear in physical form but the presence stayed with me.

I grew accustomed to it, the sweet presence of God. I wondered how I had ever lived without it.

———

The desire to study medicine seemed to be fading. Each day, I sat down to study whatever biochemistry or physiology book was before me but the texts seemed dry and unappealing. Instead, all I really wanted to do was read the Bible. What used to be words on a page of parchment now came alive like the voice of God; my desire to read His Word was insatiable. Every word throbbed and breathed and lived, each seemed to bring me closer to Him.

Still, deep inside of me I knew couldn't abandon the course I was on to become a doctor. I couldn't throw away months of studies needlessly, so I decided to sit for my exams. I sat for my written exams in biochemistry, which I passed. When the time came for me to take my oral exams, I was nervous and my thoughts were disorganized. I knew that God was calling me into ministry -away from medicine but I kept the appointment just to follow through with what I had started.

When I received the news that I had failed the oral exams, the examiners encouraged me to study harder and retest. It was a first for them that someone who had passed on the written exams had failed in the interview portion. I thanked them all but when I walked out of the room, I realized that I was relieved.

I took the failure in the oral exams as proof that my heart had changed; that I should close the door completely on my path to be a doctor. I suddenly felt as if a weight had been lifted off my shoulders and I was free to pursue what I really wanted to do: study the Bible.

I decided to return to the army, to my band of brothers, the Selous Scouts. I received a warm welcome as soon as I returned.

'Keir, you can't stay away,' my fellow Scouts would tell me. 'We need you! You have to come back and help us train up the new generation.'

I agreed to be an instructor for the Selous Scouts for a while, specifically to be part of the selection process of future recruits. On the outside, I was Keir and everyone was glad I was back. Underneath my clothes, my wounds were still pink and raw in places. Memories of the raid were definitely in the forefront of my mind, but I was determined to do everything the other instructors were doing. My experience and recent history made me a legend in the soldiers' eyes and I admit I loved taking command and being a hero among them. After all, I was one of the first of the Territorial Force to be 'belted and bereted,' and my battle scars were badges of honor in their eyes.

One day I took a troop of young soldiers to the rifle range to zero their weapons (to ensure that they were on target and their sights were aligned for targets). It was a beautiful day, and the men set up targets against an earthen bank. The Land Rover carrying the ammunition and other necessities, was parked close by.

As soon as the men put up their targets and retreated, I began the command sequence:

'Clear weapons!' The men removed empty magazines from their AK-47s and FNs.

I went down the line, checking each weapon to see if it had been done properly. All appeared to be good, so I told them to place their weapons on the ground and load a magazine of twenty rounds. Everything was routine; these were seasoned soldiers who had done this many times.

'Load!'

'Engage your target in your own time. Five rounds each!'

Suddenly, the field erupted in gunfire and I jumped, terrified. Instantly, I was transported back to the day I was wounded. My heart raced; I could smell cordite fumes and the diesel coming from the Land Rover. My first impulse was to dive under the Landie to take cover, but I forced myself to be a soldier. I grabbed my AK-47, which was leaning against the vehicle, grabbed a full magazine of ammunition from the back and took two strides to an open position next to the last soldier. I loaded my weapon, cocked it and shot at the earthen bank at random. The fear in me subsided and my breathing steadied. The adrenaline that set my pulse thumping and deafened my ears slowly faded.

Suddenly, I was aware that I was surrounded by silence. I looked up and saw all the soldiers staring back at me. I remembered that I was the instructor in charge of this group; for a few seconds I had been out of it. I looked down the line of men standing with their weapons pointing in the air.

The soldier nearest to me was looking at me, strangely. 'Sir, what are you doing?'

I was surprized at the question but even more at the look on his face. He had every right to ask the question but I still wanted to appear authoritative.

I turned to face him and then took a step forward. 'I am with you. Clear your weapons.' As the sounds of weapons being cleared reverberated, I proceeded to walk down the line of soldiers again, making sure the weapons were clear before we inspected the groupings on the targets.

Yes, I was with them again; I was myself again. I don't know how, but I had made the right choice. The painful memory of what happened was real, but I resorted to the training that I was given as a Scout.

This encounter with myself was a lesson of huge value to me later. Wounds heal. One has to pick up where one leaves off or else you continue to circle the mountain of pain and memories. I've heard that soldiers who have survived wounding are the most dangerous men in the field because they have faced death already. Just as my physical wounds were healing, I realized there was a deeper wound in my soul that also needed to be healed.

I would have lived in the vicious throes of post-traumatic stress if I hadn't come face to face with Jesus that day when my friend Dennis asked me to come to church with him.

———

During the last two years I spent in the military, I began doing what can only be described as ministry in the field. Salvation had come to me mightily but I was still responsible as a sergeant major in the Selous Scouts. I grew more confident every day, knowing that God was with me. I carried a little Gideon's Bible in my left breast pocket; part of my weaponry that I would put on even before my gun and my ammunitions belt. I knew that I was Christ's and He had a concern not only for me, but also for all the soldiers in the field.

Because I was reading the Bible in the field during my down time, the Word of God was permeating my heart and changing my focus. The book of James and Psalm 91 especially seemed to have been written just for me:

> *'He who dwells in the shelter of the Most High*
> *Will abide in the shadow of the Almighty.*
>
> *I will say to the Lord, 'My refuge and my fortress,*
> *My God, in whom I trust!'*
> *For it is He who delivers you from the snare of the trapper*
> *And from the deadly pestilence.*
>
> *He will cover you with His pinions,*
> *And under His wings you may seek refuge;*
> *His faithfulness is a shield and bulwark.*
> *You will not be afraid of the terror by night,*
> *Or of the arrow that flies by day;Of the pestilence that stalks in darkness,*
> *Or of the destruction that lays waste at noon.*

A thousand may fall at your side
And ten thousand at your right hand,
But it shall not approach you.
You will only look on with your eyes

And see the recompense of the wicked.
For you have made the Lord, my refuge,
Even the Most High, your dwelling place.
No evil will befall you,
Nor will any plague come near your tent.

For He will give His angels charge concerning you,
To guard you in all your ways.
They will bear you up in their hands,
That you do not strike your foot against a stone.
You will tread upon the lion and cobra,
The young lion and the serpent you will trample down.

'Because he has loved Me, therefore I will deliver him;
I will set him securely on high,
  because he has known My name.
'He will call upon Me, and I will answer him;
I will be with him in trouble;
I will rescue him and honor him.
'With a long life I will satisfy him
And let him see My salvation.'

I was captivated by His Father heart for me, completely trusting His direction. Here was our country on the verge of collapse, I was a soldier fighting terrorism – and I was unafraid. I was convinced that God had us all in the palm of His hands.

I started to see the miraculous taking place all around me.

On one occasion I was involved with 'Operation Miracle' – simply named because to accomplish this op would take a miracle. During the evening I could sense that God was calling me to minister His authority over the whole field.

I boldly walked up to a Captain, nestled in a trench in the half-light. The cold night was coming and he was with his troops, ready for battle. The smell of smoke was everywhere, coming from bombs landing around us.

I looked him straight in the eye and asked him, 'Sir, are you okay?'

He looked back at me, knowing I had a word for him. Still, he was a

Captain and I was a lesser rank. Selous Scout or not, he wasn't going to share his concerns or fears with me. 'Yes, I am, Sergeant Major. Why would you ask?'

'Well, sir. I just want to pray for you.'

He squirmed a bit, but agreed. 'Alright.'

I laid my hand on his shoulder and I began: 'Lord, take care of this man, preserve him. Let your protection, especially Psalm 91 be over him as a banner. Let him walk in faith after this, knowing that You are real and that there is an absolute truth that is found in You.'

He looked up at me and I knew that the authority of God had him. I stood up and walked away. We got airbursts of RPG-7s over us at a distance of 750 meters. Exploding bombs surrounded us, but none of them hit us. That night, it was as if there was an invisible canopy over us, protecting us from harm.

I started developing a reputation as one who was always praying for people. I had soldiers come to me under cover of darkness, asking for prayer. It was a delight to pray for them, it was all that mattered. I eventually realized that God was at work everywhere and that He always had been. I was now just wide-awake and realizing how powerful He is.

The book of James told me to consider it pure joy when we face trials of many kinds. I considered it a joy to be in the army, in the battle-field. I loved being with men who were wanting and needing salvation. I have many memories of whispering the prayers of salvation in the battlefield where men didn't know if they would last through the night. I remember their voices and their desperation as they prayed; I remember the peace that followed.

My best memories of the army are of those last two years. The dangers of battle were eclipsed by the power of God and His salvation.

———

I finally decided to take a leap of faith and apply for Bible School so that I could get a theological degree; it was what I had been yearning for. I applied to Christ For The Nations Institute (a Bible school with a reputation for training students in over 120 nations and building up churches all over the world) in the hopes that I would be accepted.

I was a little concerned about telling Callie – especially as the base was in Dallas, Texas in the USA. We had put Jenni, our beloved first-born, into a crèche when she was very young because Callie had had to work while I was in medical school. Now I had left medical school and I had this hare-brained notion of packing up and going off to America to attend Bible school. She wouldn't complain; that's not what I was concerned about. Callie was always very supportive and wanted only to support me as I pursued my life's destiny. The problem was that I had already taken her on a wild ride in our marriage and I didn't want to break her heart. I knew we wouldn't agree about attending Bible School – not one bit.

Our pastor at the time was Tim Salmon. I confided in him all of the things the Lord had been showing me. He was encouraging, saying that he saw the same call of God on my life that I was sensing. In his enthusiasm, he greeted Callie at church one day to voice his approval.

'Congratulations, Callie!' he beamed on Sunday morning. Callie was nonplussed. The only thing she thought he might be talking about was her secret expectant-mother status.

'How did you know I was pregnant?' she asked, shyly.

Tim laughed. 'Well, congratulations on that, too! I was talking about the other new change in your life: Keir going to Bible School in America? How impressive! Are you going to enroll too?'

Callie describes what every wife can (at one time or another) describe as a screeching halt in her heart. The urge to say 'WHAT!?? My husband hasn't informed ME of this major life change! How do you know?' had to be controlled. She looked around for me, wondering what was going on. It was an awkward moment, to say the least.

There was an icy silence in the car that morning as we drove home. ('Don't talk to me! Don't touch me!') Callie was devastated that I hadn't shared my heart with her as I had with Tim. Later that night, there was a plain and simple conversation. Bible School was not an option right now. Callie was pregnant and we had a young daughter. Even if we had the funds (which we didn't) it was an impossibility to expect to go off to a foreign country and begin Bible School. We would have to uproot ourselves, children and all, to go and chase another dream - one that might not even work out.

That evening we spoke in a very matter-of-fact way. There was no fight; there were no harsh words or accusations. I realized that the desire and the vision were not going to happen right away. I would have to pray and ask God what direction to take now.

That evening, after Callie went to bed, I prayed. It was a simple and desperate prayer: 'God, if you're calling me into full-time ministry, you'd better call Callie as well. I would rather that you call us BOTH, so that we can BOTH be responsible to YOU – she will not just be a dutiful wife being responsible to me. I will not manipulate her into this and I will trust you to speak to her as you spoke to me. I also know that you will have to provide the funds and the school and the desire.'

I slept well that night, knowing that God had it all in His hands.

Not long after that, Callie went to her regular ladies' Bible Study group. It just so happened that the lesson was all about 'submission' — a dreaded topic for most women to both teach and hear. Callie listened and took it to heart but it wasn't anything she hadn't heard before.

As she was driving home, however, the presence of God came upon her mightily. His presence was so strong that she had to pull her car over to the side of the road and stop. Under the strong presence, she wept as she felt surrounded by love as He spoke to her.

'If you will submit to Keir, then Keir can submit to ME - and fulfill the call I have on both of your lives. Acknowledge the fact that he does want to go to Bible school, then I will call BOTH of you and you'll never lack provision.'

The words were definitely spoken by God and Callie was instantly changed deep in her heart. Later that day, she came to me and shared. She agreed to submit to the call that God had on both of our lives to go to Bible School; she wanted to be part of the 'calling' that God had told her about. She was humbled, excited for the future but still apprehensive about the location.

'Keir,' she cried. 'Please let's not go away to America. I don't want to leave this place. I have a supportive network here with my friends and family. I know this is God, but it's a hard calling and I don't want to do it.' She knew it was God's calling on her life and my life as well and that evening she wept as she realized the cost of following God.

I picked her up into my arms and comforted her. Anyone who is married knows how hard this moment must have been for me – we were about to venture into uncharted territory. Even with my wife crying in my arms and a desire to protect her from all harm, I knew that obedience to God would be where we found our peace.

'Callie,' I said. 'This is the best thing for us.'

My truth and Callie's truth were second to God's righteous truth. He was definitely calling us into a deeper place, one where we would be tested and sculpted and forged into weapons in His hands. I thought we were as ready as we needed to be.

———

Rhodesia finally succumbed to inevitable change in February 1980. Under pressure from US Secretary of State Henry Kissinger, the Prime Minister of South Africa B. J.Vorster persuaded Ian Smith to accept that white minority rule could not continue in Rhodesia. The two 'Patriotic Front' groups under Mugabe would prevail and Rhodesia became Zimbabwe-Rhodesia. With the simple stroke of a pen and a piece of paper sliding across a desk - it was done.

Many of the Special Forces groups were told by their commanding officers to leave the country as there could be bloodshed. Many of my fellow soldiers did leave, scattering far and wide. We remained since Callie was by then nine months pregnant.

I will never forget the day that Simon was born: 6 March 1980. The skies were silent. No more sounds of choppers and military planes flying about. It was a bittersweet time for me, overshadowed by the birth of our new child, it seemed to be the dawn of a new day in our lives too.

Many of our friends flocked to South Africa, fearing the changes happening in Zimbabwe-Rhodesia. During this time, we readied ourselves to go to school for ministry. It was what God was calling me into, even though I didn't use those words.

Simon was five months old when we packed up our things. Our parents didn't really understand why I was doing all of this. They understood that I was an adventurer and a pilgrim; the change suited me. But Callie? How could you do this, Keir? Taking Callie away from her family and friends across the ocean with two young children?

We tried to explain. Even Callie told them that it wasn't me who was calling her away, it was God. My Father was her Father; He was call-ing both of us. They finally agreed to support us; they weren't really happy but they supported us. We had been granted full student's visas by the United States and we were allowed in to attend Bible school. Not only had we both been accepted into Christ For The Nations Institute, we received full scholarships. All we would have to pay for would be our room and board. This would be a challenge – our monthly support was 100 Zimbabwean dollars.

We boarded that airplane with only our suitcases and our two children: Simon (five months) and Jenni (three years). We had given away everything we owned except for one trunk-full of our most precious possessions. It cost us everything to obey but we did so gladly, knowing we had heard God. There was no greater satisfaction in our hearts than our mutual desire to obey Him. It would be the first ocean flight we would make as a couple for the sake of the Gospel, an incredible step of faith.

The truth of our calling was that God had called us both into something that knew no boundaries. We were in for the adventure of our lives.

This chapter is called Righteous Truth, referring to this portion of the full armor of God. The belt of truth holds everything in place; the breastplate of righteousness and the sword of the Spirit are both held in place by the belt of truth. The one and only truth is the Word of God – the Bible.

God's Word has to be a living experience with me - not man's opinions, not perspectives interpreted through a commentary. It has to be His Word, His direction. Over the years I have experienced massive peer pressure (even in the church!) to conform to the way others think but I am a man who listens to one commander – anything else would be treason.

Men feel uncomfortable functioning in someone else's revelation. Unless you are able to wear your own belt, the one that fits your waist, it will feel foreign to you. David was asked to wear Saul's armor but he couldn't walk in it; he was uncomfortable in it. David was built to be a giant killer and the reason he killed the giant was because he saw the Ark of the Covenant in a Philistine's house and the giant was in the way. He went through the giant to get to the presence of God – that was the most important thing.

In my life I have wanted the presence of God more than anything.

After all, He made Himself known to me when I was wounded; I wanted Him back permanently. I wanted to be with Him forever, to be alive in His presence. To stay there, my heart had to be set on the Word of truth and nothing more. It was the same Word that my father read to me as a young lad, it was the Word that I cried out when I was dying.

When I cried out for God's presence, His truth, it wasn't like I had been taught in church. There were no holy choirs of angels singing or harp music but a violent outburst coming from me for Him and His presence. 'From the days of John the Baptist until now, the kingdom of heaven has been subjected to violence and violent people have been raiding it…' (Matthew 11:12) It was the violence of truth that settled in my heart. So since God set it in me, I vowed that no man could ever upset me.

It was the Word of God that I was thirsty for in battle and in medical school. With my body and mind I had to pursue it. When I became a soldier, I dressed in uniform as an outward sign of who I was fighting for; how I obeyed would determine the kind of soldier I was. SO it was with the Gospel: the word of truth set in my heart but I had to train my mind and body to obey it. My body, mind and spirit had to match up with the call of God, the call that Callie and I responded to. Because of His truth, I know with absolute certainty who I am and who I fight for.

Keir and Callie Tayler on their wedding day, 1974

4

GOSPEL OF PEACE

...And with your feet fitted with the readiness
that comes from the gospel of peace.

Ephesians 6:15 NASB

Breathe deeply. Imagine a peaceful place with you at the center. It might be a beach where the waves are lapping against the shore and you are rocking in a hammock with an ice-cold drink in your hands. It might be a forest in the shade of massive trees, the sun peeking through the canopy of leaves. It might be your mother's kitchen, your garden, or a quiet church with stained glass windows.

Your idea of a peaceful place might not be a highway clogged with dangerous rush hour traffic in a foreign country. You probably didn't imagine yourself in the kitchen, staring at an empty refrigerator, wondering if you would have enough money to feed your family. I would never imagine a peaceful place as being in bed, tossing and turning at three o'clock in the morning wondering about an uncertain future.

Our version of peace is often circumstantial – God's version of peace lies in one person: Jesus Christ.

Because our changing circumstances are chaotic, God instructs us to 'put on the shoes' of readiness. Get ready for what is about to come because you will have to negotiate some tough paths. He is our peace -not a place, not circumstances, but a person. Jesus Christ becomes the hammock and the frosty beverage in the middle of rush hour traffic.

———————

Our initial experience in America and the way I had envisioned it, were worlds apart. When we arrived at the Bible school, we moved in to what we had thought would be a furnished apartment. Before us were blank walls and plain carpets dotted with a few pieces of furniture left behind by the previous tenants. There were no beds, no bedding, not even plates to eat off. I had to run to McDonald's to get cutlery to eat our dinner with that first night.

We put our five month old, Simon, in a bureau drawer that first night so that he could sleep in a secure little cot. Our beloved Jenni slept on the floor. Callie and I scrambled over the next few days to get a few pieces of furniture together, relying heavily on donations. We managed to get a bed for ourselves and one for Jenni. A playpen served as a cot for Simon. We were expected to start attending classes in a few days and we still had to make a home out of a bare apartment and arrange childcare for the children.

Our scholarships required that we would work for the school for five hours each day after attending classes. It was the ideal arrangement for single students who were fresh out of University but it proved to be too much for us. Callie was a young mother who had just left her home country and family and was now being asked to leave her young children with a stranger in a crèche. After a very short deliberation, we decided that Callie should simply 'audit' classes. She would be enrolled as a student in the course but not be required to turn in written assignments and would, therefore, be without the benefit of a course credit. In exchange for giving up a Bible School degree, Callie was given freedom to be a mother to her young children and a wife to me – something that she felt was the most important in the midst of all this change. She would not have to work at the end of a school day and could be a full-time mother to the kids.

We had never (in all of our married life) spent more than four months together under the same roof. For the first five years of our marriage I had been a soldier, always being called out on a mission. I was delighted to be coming home at the end of the day to our sparsely furnished apartment to see my beautiful family, all happy to see me. We could do things like eat dinner together and maybe go for a walk or visit with friends. We had very little money, but it was nonetheless a happy time. After all, we were together living the dream of following God's will for our lives. It was amazing.

From a young age, Jenni and Simon were immersed in a church culture – they were trained up in the Bible and there was a beauty and safety in that. Jenni had her own circle of friends that loved her dearly. She began speaking with an American accent within three weeks of being there.

There were 1 400 students at Bible School and about thirty families had come from Zimbabwe. We were the biggest contingent of foreign nationals at the Bible school, so Callie and I had quite a lot of friends once we arrived. I think the Americans thought we all knew each other back in Zim, but we didn't. God had released us all to go into ministry at the same time and, since we all knew about the years of war and chaos that had happened back in our homeland, we were all ready to become ministers of the Gospel of peace.

America was a very different climate; it had a very different culture. In Zim we had to queue to get toothpaste or toilet paper, in America there was an abundance of everything. People used to eye Callie and me as we shopped in the supermarket as if we were aliens (and we were!) The choices were endless and we had to make decisions about brands and compare prices. It was a challenge we hadn't expected – there were so many ways to feel lost and confused. Many times we came away from shopping exhausted, our heads spinning and with an empty cart!

The American students didn't seem to know much about our country or the upheaval we had just been through. No one seemed to know much about the war or Rhodesia becoming Zimbabwe. No one knew what a Selous Scout was ('Is that like a Boy Scout?' they would ask me.) I had no identity, no reputation. I was just Keir from Africa ('why aren't you black?')

Since African homes are not usually close to a main road, it was hard for me to grow accustomed to street noises while I slept. One night a vehicle passed by our apartment and backfired as it slowed down. I instantly grabbed Callie and rolled off the bed onto the floor, panting as the adrenaline rushed through my veins. I thought our family was under attack; the only time I had heard noises like that before was during the war. Only when I realized I was safe did I allow my poor wife to get back into bed and continue sleeping. The reactions to certain stimuli still lived within me; fourteen years of war did not fade overnight, even after I had crossed an ocean.

I was now in a first world country that from most people's perspective was superior to mine. It made no sense that we missed our home so much, but we did. We missed our families, the landscape: the wild nights and the open doors. The sounds of the bush were not present where we were; neither was the wildlife that inhabited it.

Even more noticeable was our change in identity. Our new life required us to lose whatever we esteemed in ourselves (good or bad) and to rest in the fact that we belonged to God. Our identity is sacred to us; it is what makes us individuals, so this was a painful time for Callie and me in many ways.

Many nights I would lie awake, thinking that I was lost in a sea of people who didn't know me or didn't respect what God had done in me. Our only chance of surviving and not becoming bitter, lay in remembering that God was our Father and we were His children. I was a stranger in a strange land and for the first time, I realized what Callie had voiced her concern about – starting over completely from scratch and becoming a new creation to myself and others. He would comfort me during those times:

'Keep the things I've taught you,' He would tell me. 'Remember I have brought you here to know my word and Me. Keep learning; keep seeking. I'm going to place in you inward strategies and a new identity. Remain close to me and I will do the work.'

I was no longer Keir the hero, Keir the medicine man, Keir the prayer warrior. It was this way for two years: I was Keir, Mr Nobody; Keir, the son of God and nothing more.

———

We attended Beverly Hills Baptist Church in Dallas while in America, a church I loved and valued. It was a blessing to be able to sit under the leadership and to hear some of the best evangelical speakers on the face of this earth. They became our family there and it was an incredible privilege for me to learn the word of God five days a week at CFNI and to have weekends at Beverley Hills Baptist. While we attended the church a strange thing happened. There was an announcement that the deacons had fired the Pastor. Callie and I were stunned; we were relatively new to churches so we didn't know that this could happen.

It was devastating to the church. Before our eyes we witnessed half the people leave while the other half remained. We would later learn this was called a 'church split' – I had heard nothing of this in the Bible. I wondered inside why all this pain should happen in a church. Somehow, we survived and carried on. The church became 'Beverley

Hills Church' – we changed our signs and our logo. We did the only thing we knew how to do; we met on Sunday mornings and wor-shipped God.

Bible School lasted for two years, with me attending classes at Christ for the Nations Institute and working for five hours a day afterwards to 'pay' for the scholarship. I took every Bible survey and theology course the school offered and I loved it. I also taught our church, as well as training their football team (off season) by lifting weights and incorporating military knowledge and skills. It was a delight for me, it reminded me of being a sergeant major in the Scouts, guiding new soldiers into becoming fit.

I was listening to the Word of God every day. Other courses such as 'How to Counsel' or 'Children's Ministries' held no interest for me – I was there to study the Word of God. I drank it in deeply and let it fill my heart and mind.

As a family, Callie and I got into a routine and lived carefully during those years. We now knew the foods that we liked and could afford - our budget would allow only a few extravagances. We had a close circle of friends that we socialized with regularly; we went on week-end trips together. It was a good time in our lives.

On one occasion our family had only twenty American dollars left; all we had in the world until I received my stipend. We were moved with compassion one night for one of our friends who had a great need, so we gave him ten of those dollars. Feeling a little giddy about it afterwards, Callie and I impulsively decided to go out for a romantic dinner across the street to McDonalds. As we were sneaking out of our apartment (with a babysitter within distracting our children), the phone rang. I wondered whether to answer it and decided to do so. On the other end was a pastor friend of mine by the name of John Katchik. Callie and I had recently been into his church and shared our testimony.

'Hello is that brother Tayler?'

'Yes sir, it is'.

'Our church has just had a missions meeting. Our whole staff has taken a vote and we've decided to support you and your family with one hundred and ten dollars a month for the duration of your stay at

CFNI. I want you to know the first check is in the mail to you.'

I felt my hand go numb holding the phone. One hundred and ten American dollars! I could barely contain my surprize and joy!

Well - we had dinner that night!

We had many such experiences. Just as He promised us, our life was lived on the edge but we never lacked anything. Because He is who He is though, He decided to add joy, surprizes and 'SUDDENLYs!'

One such 'suddenly' happened in the spring of my second year at CFNI. While I was still a student I had the privilege of delivering mail to the different staff members and apartment blocks for the students. This enabled me to get into the offices of all the professors - some of who I built a good relationship with. I loved this perk! No appointments, no permission…'Just your mail getting delivered, Professor – and by the way may I ask a question about that lecture?'

I worked on campus, which meant going back and forth from freezing rain outside to warm buildings inside. I was a little negligent and I came down with pneumonia and had to go to hospital. Simon, our little son, was not well either and we were both there (without medical insurance) waiting for a doctor to see us.

I was told that I had pneumonia but because I had no financial means the hospital couldn't admit me, nor would they accept the liability of telling me I could leave. I can remember lying on the emergency room bed and Callie holding Simon, limp with fever. We decided to pray.

'Lord help us,' I pleaded. 'We are in your hands.'

Within minutes, a nurse called Callie to the counter.

'Mrs Tayler we have some interesting news,' she said. 'The administrator of CFNI, Mr Leon Cornelius, has just called to tell me that he is prepared to pay all your expenses here. Keir can be admitted'.

 Callie froze and rejoiced at the same time. 'What about Simon?' she asked.

'We will put him on a dose of antibiotics and let him go home with you,' she said. 'Children do better when they are allowed to return to their cozy homes.'

Well, we rejoiced!

While I was in the hospital, Callie came in to visit me with both of our children in tow. I could see with my own eyes that Simon was much improved, but there was a concern on Callie's face. She came close to my bed and looked at me straight in the eye.

'Keir, I have something to tell you and it's not good,' she said. Her eyes were filling with tears. 'Your Mum has just passed away.'

I felt a bolt of lightning hit my heart but Callie continued. 'Your Dad and Mum were having tea together on the farm this morning, just like they always do. Your Dad was reading the Bible to her and as he passed her a cup of tea, he noticed that she didn't take it from him. She had gone. The verse your Dad had been reading was '…into thy hands I commit my spirit."

I swallowed hard; Callie could tell I was grief stricken and hugged me tightly. 'Keir I am so sorry to bring this to you now.'

What could I do? I knew I had to release all this into God's hands. My Mum knew salvation, and I would see her again, I was sad I wouldn't see her on earth and I admit it was such a shock. I was so torn knowing that I would never see her again on our farm in Rhodesia, never hear her voice again, feel her tender looks; but she was home.

Callie and I were drawn closer together at this time; she became the definition of 'my family.'

I cried, I prayed, I rejoiced, I was silent.

Eventually, I recovered.

As our time in Bible School drew to a close, Callie and I wondered what we should do. We knew we had to return to Zimbabwe (our student visas were about to expire) but we didn't know how God would be using us once we got there. I had no invitations from churches to be part of their leadership, which I had thought would be the case. Our future seemed uncertain until I got a call from Tim Salmon, our former pastor in Zim, inviting us to be part of a church he had planted in Pietermaritzburg, South Africa. The church had its own gymnasium and they needed an elder on staff who could also function as a gym trainer. Tim instantly thought of me and asked me to give it some thought.

It didn't take much thought. After all, Tim was the pastor who sent us off to Bible school. He cared deeply for us and for our future; he also recognized my gifting. Although the church was in Pietermaritzburg, South Africa, I was up for the challenge. I accepted the invitation and told him we would come to him as soon as we could and that we would be in touch. I was ready to return to Africa and so was Callie. We were ready to bring our kids back into the world that was once our home.

By the time I graduated from school, I realized that I was a completely different person from the Keir who enrolled. I had spent two years living in complete faith that God would provide for us. I lived in America as an alien, a person of no reputation. I learned to listen to the voice of God, who led me as I followed.

Bible school wasn't only an academic process for me; I transitioned there from a soldier to a son.

———

We made an exit strategy (which wasn't complicated) and like children, we doled out our few possessions among the friends we had there and loved so much. We knew that how we left America would greatly influence how we entered Zimbabwe – especially in ministry. Beverley Hills Church, now being led by Jim Hodges, Mike Massa and Dutch Sheets, gave us a going away party. We cried as we left this precious family who had accepted Callie and me and our children as their own. They gave us a gift, two thousand American dollars, which we desperately needed. We understood their sacrifice and that made it was even more touching. Like parents, they gave us what they could and wished us well. What we didn't give away, we packed tightly into our suitcases and then, like nomads, we prepared to retrace our steps.

We boarded our plane and waited for takeoff, but it never came. Instead, we were delayed again and again. Finally, a flight attendant came on the loudspeaker:

'Ladies and Gentlemen, I'm sorry to do this to you, but our flight is not going to leave today. Please gather your belongings; leave nothing behind and exit the plane.'

There were no further instructions; it was very strange. People were wondering what else they should do or where their connecting flights were going to be. The flight attendants had no answers for us; even they looked concerned. We exited and the airport scene was absolute chaos. Angry people were crowded around the ticket counters, impatiently demanding to be reassigned.

We found out that the aircraft was the property of Braniff airlines, which now ceased to exist. They had declared bankruptcy and grounded all of their flights. There was no plan to reassign passengers, let alone reimburse them. Passengers seemed to be filled with panic, people behind the counters were walking away since they were no longer employed. We were all left clutching worthless tickets, stranded in a crowded airport and not knowing where to turn. I looked at Callie and my children; we hadn't even packed sandwiches to eat on the plane. I had a whopping forty American dollars in my pocket, not even enough for a night's stay in a hotel. The two thousand dollars which was given to us by our church was en route to a bank account in South Africa!

As if this were not bad enough, a terrible thunderstorm broke out over Dallas and the airport was choked with passengers from flights that could not leave. It was like a nightmare when you are fully awake. People were hostile and unfriendly on top of being displaced. We went back to CFNI and stayed with friends in the apartments. They were sympathetic to our plight but we were all students with very little cash. We did what we knew how to do: we prayed.

We were stranded for a week. Our tickets were for Dallas to London, then London to Salisbury (soon to be re-named Harare). We watched news reports, called the airlines, went to business offices, waited for someone. We pleaded our case as best we could: we were a young family whose American visas were about to expire. We had no money to pay for flights and we wanted to take the first plane home. The airlines could do very little; after all, Braniff had ceased to exist. They had no customer service department and no counter at the airport.

Finally, one of our friends came to us with the results of a very diligent search. There was a written clause in The IATA regulations, a 'fine print agreement', that stated that if the airline we held tickets with was unable to perform its duties, then any foreign passenger was entitled to have seats on another plane whose route was similar (Dallas to London to Salisbury). If this were true, we were basically entitled to a free ticket out of the country to return home. We decided to pack up and take our chances at the airport again.

We found the first flight with that route: American Airlines. When we approached them with this new information, the man behind the counter instructed the ticket agent:

'Give them any seats they want.'

He walked away and I stammered. I didn't know what to do, so I shot for the moon: 'Can we have the bulkhead seats because we have small children?'

The ticket agent typed to see if the seats were available, then nodded. There was a clattering as the tickets were printed and then (angel choir singing) our family moved through the security line and boarded a plane for home. I was so relieved, so happy. All of our prayers had been answered and I was flooded with gratitude… until I had a thought: *I should have asked for Business Class.*

We arrived in Zimbabwe and straightaway went to my Dad's farm. It was wonderful to return to the place where I grew up, but strange without my mother there. While Callie and I were accustomed to the wild, my children had grown up in the concrete jungle of Dallas, Texas, where the only wildlife were the children running through a man-made park with slides and swings.

Simon was now three years old and when he arrived, he regarded the soil as if it was a special treasure. He let the sandiness of it run through his fingers; he wanted to taste it. There was a period of about thirty minutes where the kids regarded the forest with apprehension; then they embraced it, running wild and barefoot and free, just like I had as a child.

Then, like true Taylers, they became obsessed with exploring. I didn't see them much for three days. They were always off after breakfast, scouting out new and exciting hiding places and territories. Callie and I were delighted to see them come alive as we were.

Welcome home to Africa.

'Jesus was going through all the cities and villages, teaching in their synagogues and proclaiming the gospel of the kingdom, and healing every kind of disease and every kind of sickness. Seeing the people, He felt compassion for them, because they were distressed and dispirited like sheep without a shepherd. Then He said to His disciples, 'The harvest is plentiful, but the workers are few. Therefore beseech the Lord of the harvest to send out workers into His harvest.'

~*Matthew 9:35-38*

Jesus said this with COMPASSION, the Bible says. He sees the distressed and dispirited and feels compassion for them because they are like sheep without a shepherd. I think He knew that even in churches there is not enough encouragement for people to function in their true callings. There they should be able to reach their potential – the high place He has called them up to.

For me, I had always loved church life, even though it had been challenging. I hadn't yet felt the displacement of not walking in my calling, not finding a place of value. When our family came back to Africa, Callie and the kids stayed in Zim and I went on to South Africa, to Pietermaritzburg, to take the job as gym instructor for the church. Unfortunately, when I arrived there our pastor told me that the gym instructor idea had never really materialized. By the time Callie and the kids arrived, I had to tell her that things weren't exactly the way we had been told they would be.

As if this were not enough, I came down with a very serious case of Hepatitis and was bedridden for about six weeks. The church went through a split over finances and our new church family hardly had the time or the energy to care for us. The house we were given to rent had a toilet outside, which was a big change for our family. With two young children and a sick husband, Callie had to manage all of this and not even have a bathroom inside her own house!

It was enough to destroy our faith and call.

Somehow Callie picked up the reins and pioneered us through these unstable times. God was with all of us, sustaining us and feeding us by the spoonful. In a couple of months, I was walking again and we were slowly able to integrate into the church.

God's favor was on us.

———

One Sunday morning Tim Salmon, our pastor, told Callie and I he had a job for us; the first job we would have on staff at the church.

'There are thirty kids here and we have nothing for them,' he told us, sadly. 'Why not see what you can do?'

I was floored; this was not why I came to Pietermaritzburg. While I realized the importance of children's ministry, I never expected to inherit this task. In Bible school I took every course pertaining to

theology and ministry but I never bothered to study children's pro-
grammes. So, I panicked.

I ended up traveling to Rhema Church in Johannesburg to meet a
woman named Ruby Steenkamp, an aficionado of children's ministry.
I watched her lead the children's ministry at that church, which was
rather large and decided to follow her lead.

I came back to our church with these new ideas and strategies but I
realized that I was Keir, not Ruby. I devoted myself to the children's
ministry completely (we called it the Rainbow Children's Church)
becoming deeply involved and loving it. Not only was I in charge of
vacation Bible school and Sunday morning celebration for the kids,
but I also arranged camps and outdoor adventures for them. Blend-
ing the military experience I had into fun lessons for kids proved to
be the key to our church growing. Other people in the church volunteered to come alongside me and run the ministry.

The population of children grew from 30 to over 300 every Sunday
morning. The kids could not wait to get there; subsequently their
parents came with them. Our pastor was very happy with me; the
growth was staggering in his eyes. Before I knew it, I had trained up
an army of volunteers; when a ministry is fun, everyone wants to
volunteer.

———

I read constantly in those days, especially books by T.L. Osborne and
F. F. Bosworth, both of whom influenced me greatly. Osborn was an
American Pentecostal evangelist and author who used to preach
to great hordes of people in India. Somehow I managed to get my
hands on a collection of sermons which were stirring and powerful.
I noticed they were punctuated with dashes where the interpreter
would speak. Here was a man who would preach to audiences of 10
000 people in the open air and then pray for people and there was
healing! Nothing was more exciting to me and I felt my feet burning
with desire to go out.

With the blessing of my church, I started a 'mission's programme'
where I would take my Land Rover and go into Northern Kwazulu
Natal, with the intention of preaching the Gospel. Sometimes I'd take
two or three people with me. I loved it. I met a pastor from Mkuze
who needed help in building up his church, especially in teaching
the leaders who needed a strong Biblical foundation. He asked for

my input and I gladly sat down with him. We worked together and things came alive. In Manguzi, near the border of Mozambique, I did the same thing with some local pastors. They were overworked and needed help and I was happy to come alongside them and sort through what they needed to build Bible-based churches based on New Testament examples. It was during apartheid and sometimes the pastors seemed surprized that I was there. It was not only my privilege, but I came alive like at no other time in my life. I felt that this is what I was born to do.

Since I hadn't grown up in South Africa, I didn't know the apartheid laws or taboos. I did, however, grow up in a racist Rhodesia. While Callie and I were in America, God worked this racist influence out of me and showed me His heart: people were people. None were substandard; we were all the same, in need of Christ.

I didn't know how to express it then but T.L. Osborne was witnessing with my spirit and encouraging the call of God in my life to be an evangelist. Evangelism – the word itself means 'the spreading of the Christian gospel by public preaching or personal witness.' It occurred to me that this is what God was calling me into that very day I was saved in my church. When I looked back at the altar, He made it clear that I would be preaching.

When I returned from trips to Zululand, I would share in church what had happened. Other people wanted to come with me, so I would take teams in to ignite the same fire that had been started in me. The calling God had on my life started to come into focus and I knew I needed to respond even further.

Around this time Callie gave birth to our third child, our baby Lisa. It was as if God knew that we needed her to make us a complete family. We all loved her and considered her an absolute joy; it was the crowning glory of our life in Pietermaritzburg.

Looking back, I can see that every time God gave us a child ,He was telling us that something in our lives was about to change. The natural birth whispered of a spiritual birth that was about to happen; God was leading us further and further, deeper and deeper into His plan.

I took a trip to Botswana with our pastor, Tim. While there, I shared with him all that was going on in my heart.

'You know,' I told him. 'As much as I enjoy leading the children's ministries I think I'm ready to hand the baton to someone else.'

'Why do you say that?' he asked me.

'It seems like the guys in there can do it better than I can. I want to focus more on evangelism on a broader scale and it's a good time to get started.'

I explained as well as I could the calling of the evangelist and how I wanted to go out. In my mind, it was more than having a 'mission's ministry' – it was a way of life that was calling me. I desired to live on the edge and bring the gospel to remote places, regardless of the climate or conditions. I wanted to go anywhere for the gospel; I wanted to share the good news with people regardless of race, economic status or tribal association. A fire burned in me to be released as an approved workman bearing the gospel.

Tim suggested that I should travel with Ron Kussmaul, (an American missionary in Africa) a man who had been driving land cruisers and flying aircraft to bring the gospel all over Africa 'from the equator to Table Mountain'. Tim and Ron knew each other and apparently, the last time they had spoken, Ron had mentioned that he would love to have me on his team because I seemed rough and ready (my military experience was always seen as an asset) and I had a good knowledge of Africa.

I agreed that meeting with Ron Kussmaul would be a good idea but the man was always on the go and I didn't know when he would be able to meet with me. Tim immediately made his way to a phone to contact Ron, who went out of his way to meet us at the airport. It was only a brief conversation, but it was one that would change my life. He and I had a common vision, one to reach the unreached in Africa. A lot of people in remote villages were mixing the gospel with ancestral practices or common legends. The real gospel, the unadulterated Word of God was, however, being received well by rural Africans and they had one request: bring us more.

Within a few days, Callie and I were looking for a place to live in Harare, Zimbabwe where we were to run a forward base for Ron Kussmaul Ministries. Miraculously, we found a home very close to Callie's family. We found a car, a school for the children and settled in peace, knowing that God had arranged the whole thing.

I began working with Ron for one reason: to bring the Gospel of Jesus Christ. He had been doing it for some time and I loved travelling with him. We went into the Zambezi valley, into the war torn areas of Mozambique (whose civil war had been raging for years), through Tete and Malawi, under military escort. Many times the conditions were dangerous; on a few occasions I heard the whistle of RPG-7 rockets flying by me. Sometimes I brought back the Land Cruiser and showed Ron where paint had been chipped off by fragments of rocks hitting it, impact from an explosion. For me, it was an exciting time and I loved it.

———

The Mukumbura region of Zimbabwe was a place I wanted to go to preach. Growing up, I knew the people there suffered heavily living only a stone's throw away from the landmine-infested border of Zimbabwe and Mozambique. Poor herdsmen there lost what little livestock they had to old landmines that lay just underneath the soil. On many occasions people were also injured. Where there is grief there is also a need for salvation; also a need for healing. The problem of going into this area was not only the mines, but also that the people were naturally very untrusting of strangers. It became known as a no man's land lying between the two countries and I longed for a strategy to break into the area.

One morning, in our garden, Callie and I were praying for this region. Between us, there was a map of the area.

'Lord, please bring us a man who can take us into Mukumbura. You know who he is, Lord. Let him be known to us. We trust you to show us.'

We had no sooner stopped praying than a man staggered into our yard, old and thin and carrying a small bag. Callie and I put down our teacups and went to him.

'Can I help you, sir?' I asked. I could see the man was weak, possibly from hunger. Callie went to get him some food straightaway.

'Is this your vehicle?' he asked me.

'Yes,' I told him. I was concerned he would fall down any minute, he was so unsteady.

'I've been looking for this vehicle for three days,' he said and then leaned against it for support; he was so frail, so thin. With care, I asked him to come and sit down and have tea with us.

Callie returned with tea and sandwiches. We patiently watched him drink and eat a bit but I couldn't help wondering what he meant about my vehicle. Our Land Cruiser was painted a slightly odd color - beige with a blue stripe down the side - and had been modified into a van. Since it looked very different from most other Land Cruisers; he had probably seen it around. But where? My mind was racing.

'Thank you,' he said when he had finished eating. It took a while for him to drink more tea and the suspense was getting to me. Finally, he explained what he meant. 'My name is Kachel Molotwa and I saw your car in a dream.'

Callie and I looked at each other, stunned. The man continued:

'I had a dream a week ago about this car,' he pointed to my Land Cruiser. 'In this dream God told me that I am supposed to find this car and take you to Mukumbura to preach the Gospel.'

The man sounded matter-of-fact, but I was astounded. It was beyond belief. How could this happen?

———

Kachel and I became a team. It was easy to work with him and I could see in no time that God had brought us together. We went into Mukumbura and he guided me to the villages that we would visit. At a critical spot, we would hang a gas lamp from a baobab tree and Kachel would begin singing. This would bring people in; sometimes as many as two hundred. After that, I would preach the gospel and people would listen. Many salvations would happen on trips like these and I was so grateful that I got to live in this wonderful calling.

'This is how it is in our culture,' Kachel would tell me around the fire at night. 'As a black man, I will listen to you but the permission must come from the chief. Permission for everything.'

We both knew that our visits were not enough for the people – they needed a place to worship. I realized that churches would need to be planted. The Word of God would need to be preached for the new believers; this could only happen with the blessing of the village chief.

In one such village in the Zambezi valley we were walking around looking for the village chief. We found him, dutifully tending his garden, hoeing rows diligently. After some greetings and formalities, I posed my question:

'You know me, don't you? You know my vehicle and my motorcycle.'

The chief nodded. People in the Zambezi valley recognized my vehicle. It was hard to miss – it always had my Honda XR200R strapped to the back of it. I was living my dream and I loved it!

'You probably know by now that I come here eight or nine times a year. We would like your permission to have a piece of land to plant a church here,' I said. 'With your blessing these people could have a place to worship God.'

The man put down his hoe and wiped his brow. 'This is a matter of importance,' he said. 'Let me first consult my ancestors.'

He started to walk away and I realized that there was another realm that I was dealing with here. I wondered how one would consult dead ancestors. I knew I was up against something greater.

That night under a tree with our gas light hanging, I preached with my whole heart. The subject was the Holy Spirit and Kachel was interpreting. I felt the people staring at me, blankly. At the end of the message, we called for the people to receive the Holy Spirit.

'Who wants to receive the Holy Spirit?' I asked boldly. Nothing. Not one sound. I wondered what happened; I had never seen such blank faces. I thought for a moment that the baobab tree had more of a response than the people listening. It was like they were frozen. There was nothing else to do but end the meeting. Everyone dispersed, leaving the meeting like nothing had happened there.

I went back to the Land Cruiser with Kachel. We were discouraged and shook our heads, wondering what had happened.

The next morning, I woke up and took a walk. I walked up and down the airstrip praying. 'Lord, what am I up against here? What must I do?'

I felt His voice answer me: 'Son, don't just talk about me. This time show them who I am and what I can do.'

I didn't know what that meant, so I said, 'Sure, Lord. What do you want to do?'

He seemed to smile as He answered: 'You'll see.'

I was excited about the meeting that night. I was also a little scared. What if I messed it up? That evening's meeting began the same way.

Kachel began singing, the people came. I preached, saying, 'Last night all of you came and listened to me preach about the person of the Holy Spirit. Tonight I'm going to introduce you to Him.' Then at the end the Lord told me a secret: 'There is one woman here today with a swollen and hot left knee. Ask her to come forward and you will see that I will heal her.'

I shouted out: 'There is a woman here who has a hot and swollen left knee. Come forward and you will be healed!'

There was a mumbling and a shuffling and about six women emerged from the crowd, some of them limping, some of them walking normally. I had them line up in the front. Then, as I walked down the line of them, I prayed feverishly. 'Lord, which one is it? Is it just one? You have to show me who it is….' Right then, I stopped in front of one woman and I knew it was her. 'It's you!' I said. 'You're the lady I'm supposed to pray for!' I knelt down in front of her and put my hands on her left knee. It was massive and hot, just as God said it would be.

'Lord, HEAL this knee. Heal it once and for all. I command all the sickness to leave in the name of Jesus Christ; I command it to go down to size! Disease you are evicted from the knee!'

I said, 'Ma'am will you walk out around there?' I pointed to the left side of the crowd. She walked where I said, hobbling at first. Then, she continued to walk, leaving the light of the gas lamp. We were all watching where she was, then from around the corner we heard an ululation ('U-LU-LU-LU-LU-LU!!!') coming from her, and then she ran back to us. Instead of stopping, she ran in the other direction, past the crowd and away from the light on the other side. She came running back, panting and exclaiming that her knee was healed.

'Listen to this white man!' she yelled. 'What he's saying is the truth. This Holy Spirit just healed me! It's true! It's true!'

The people turned their attention from her to us again, this time coming towards us, wanting to receive the Holy Spirit or healing – or both. That night, a large number of people received the touch of the Holy Spirit. Many received physical healings from ailments that had been plaguing them. It took hours, but we didn't care. It was our delight and honor to see God heal person after person; to see people begin to speak in tongues and worship break out. Over and over again people were praising God, all kinds of healing was taking place.

At the end of the night, Kachel and I sat down to our tea. It was our custom we kept with each other every night. It was late, but it didn't matter. We enjoyed the night and all of its breakthrough.

'You see, Pastor,' Kachel told me. 'We people need to see it happen before we believe. That is why we need signs and wonders. These people will now believe in Holy Spirit because of what He has done for them.'

It occurred to me that it was exactly as God had said. God wanted to minister in a different way to these people; it turns out He had a plan to reach them that was different from my formula that night. As we sat with our tea, I heard the lowing of a cow behind me. I thought that a cow had escaped from its pen (people used to pen their live-stock at night to protect them from landmines and wild animals).

As I heard it, the Lord said 'That is not a cow that is a man with a de-monic spirit in him. He is coming for you, Keir, so make yourself ready.'

I did. I put my tea down to the side and stood up with Kachel. Sure enough, a man came out of the grass, waving a white shirt above his head. His face was wild and mad, his massive body glowing brown and sweat-covered. He came toward us and stopped in front of us. He spoke up in a deep voice that didn't sound like his own – in perfect English: 'Who are you? WE are the ones here!'

I knew exactly what he was talking about; it was a manifestation of demons in this one body. Because the Holy Spirit had shown up in people and taken authority in their lives, the ancestral spirits were now challenging us. He was heaving and terrible sounds were com-ing from him, but I stood where I was and pointed at him, saying:

'NO, YOU'RE NOT! Jesus Christ is now the ruler of this place and He is the one who is here now!'

We were camped at the Police Station and the commotion caused police officers to come out, weapons ready.

'What is going on here?' They asked me. 'Is this man bothering you? Are you being harassed by him?'

I turned to them and shrugged. 'No, not really.'

I knew I was in control and had authority. The police knew it, as well; so did the possessed man. The police still took the man off and imprisoned him for the night, thinking he might pose a danger to the village if left alone.

That night, Kachel and I hardly slept at all. It was so exciting to see the village transformed by the activity of the Holy Spirit.

The next morning we went into the police station and asked about the man who had been lowing like a cow. 'He changed once we brought him in,' they told us. 'He was put in a cell and then we heard him speaking a strange language. He seems calm now; would you like to visit him?'

We said we would and we came up to the man, who seemed genuinely glad to see us. We asked him if he remembered anything about what had happened the night before. He really didn't have a great recall but he did say that once he got to his cell, he felt a presence like no other he had ever felt. The presence was one that made him realize he was surrounded by the Spirit of God and he surrendered his heart to Him.

So, that man was saved in the prison cell that night, even without deliverance or prayer for inner healing. The Holy Spirit made the man whole and the person we were talking to was clothed and in his right mind.

We ended up getting the land to build the church on. To my knowledge, that church is still operational to this day.

———

From a military perspective, peace is the end result of a war. I think this part of the armor is worn on our feet because it is how we balance ourselves; how we stand.

Jesus mentioned that word PEACE to his disciples twice when he appeared to them. He walked straight through a brick wall and said 'PEACE be with you' – he didn't challenge them other than to have PEACE. Jesus knew exactly who He was; there was never a desire to prove Himself. When you walk in peace, you walk in victory. You have absolute authority and final authority.

On the cross Jesus said, 'IT is FINISHED.' That finish is peace; He is our peace.

Put on the shoes - they are hard to walk in at first, but as you get used to them you will break them in. The definition of "shod" in the scripture is 'wearing shoes that are not removed', or shoes we don't take off every day. Once we're used to them, it feels uncomfortable without them – once we wear the shoes of the gospel, it is impossible to live without them.

Our landrovers, that took us to the nations.

5

THE IMPENETRABLE SHIELD

In addition to all this, take up the shield of faith,
with which you can extinguish all the flaming arrows of the evil one.

Ephesians 6:16

'Are you ready?'

'Yes, sir, I am.'

A simple question from the commanding officer to the soldier. There is one question and only one answer. A soldier is useless to his commanding officer if he is not ready to go at a moment's notice.

Often Ron Kussmaul would call and tell me that there was a trip taking place into a remote area in Mozambique, Zimbabwe or Malawi.

'Get everything together,' he'd say. 'I'll meet you in Blantyre.'

I'd drop whatever I was doing and I was able to have our Land Cruiser packed up and ready to go within an hour. On most trips I went on with Ron we would have a team of guys with us. We valued strong relationships, especially with our translators, knowing that they were the bridge between us and the people. Our team would go out to remote areas that desperately needed fellow leaders to help them spread the gospel. We would arrive, speak to the leaders and then address their congregations or hold a revival.

Most of the time they were indigenous black people; most of the time they were poor. These are the people who God gave me a passion for, the ones who I felt the most connected to.

Sometimes the leaders could read, sometimes they couldn't. Each time, our connection was real; our teaching was the same, the Word was unadulterated. Leaders would succeed in leading a church if they accepted the Bible as truth; if they loved the truth of the gospel.

I loved the life I was living; because of my military training I was able to be ready at a moment's notice. My family paid a heavy price while I was gone.

'Where are you off to this time, Daddy?' Jenni would ask me as I tucked her into bed.

Simon and Lisa would listen for my answer; Callie usually let me do the explaining. I'd tell them first how much I loved them and valued them. I told them how much I loved their mother and valued her and then I would tell them where I was going and why.

'Jesus Christ is my Commander-in-chief,' I'd say. 'He is the King of Kings and the creator of all things. I am chosen to go and spread the Word.' Then, depending on where I was going, I would tell them specifically where and for how long and ask for their prayers. 'He's asked me to go into the nation of Malawi this time. I'm meeting the team in Blantyre and I will be gone for three days.'

I never hid anything from them, nor did I ever sugarcoat the sacrifice we were all making for Dad to do this. I knew that my being away from home was hard for them, after all, we were a family. Sometimes after my goodbyes I would leave with tears in my eyes, knowing that they were lonely for me. I prayed fervently for God's protection over them while I was gone.

Callie and I were bulletproof- she understood the calling on my life; it was her calling too. My children, however, were so young that sometimes the cost seemed too high. Sometimes they didn't understand why we couldn't be one of those normal families they saw in church. I prayed that they would not be among the casualties of pastor's children who had fallen away from God because of my absence. It is by God's grace that we were held together.

Anyone in full-time ministry can tell you it is a family calling; not just the calling of one person.

———

One of the first lessons God ever gave me was to be humble and teachable and I have tried to remain so. Even to this day I know that ministry is a learning process in the Kingdom.

I learned a lot about the prophetic as I travelled with Ron. He had an amazing gift to hear God and minister His truth. During large crusades we would often have thousands of people at the teaching.

After the teaching there would be prayer ministry. I would stay close to Ron, hoping to learn how to sense the Spirit of God as I ministered with Ron. I positioned myself next to him whenever I could, wanting to catch what he had. He seemed to want to pass on anything he knew; he never gave the impression that what he was doing was exclusive to him.

One morning, as Ron was preaching about the Holy Spirit I was listening nearby, getting the coffee cups ready for the local pastors.

Suddenly, one of the pastors came running up to me. 'Hey, Ron wants you! He wants you to preach the message!'

'What?' I stopped what I was doing only to look back at him. 'I don't think so.' A lot of his supporters from the USA were there, wanting only to hear Ron preach.

'You had better go up there,' he said. 'You're preaching in a couple of minutes.' I made my way to the front but I wondered what to do. After all, I hadn't been paying close attention to what he was saying.

I came up to the front, stood next to Ron and listened as the translator finished his sentence.

'Are you ready?' he asked me. It was as if he was asking me to load up the Land Cruiser and suddenly, I realized that was just what he was asking. It was no different …and I was ready to preach the Good News of Jesus Christ. After all, I was living it. Ron handed me the mike.

'Yes, sir.' I answered.

I had to catch up; where was he? Then, an amazing thing happened. I started preaching without fear. I started to talk about how the Holy Spirit was with us always and that He was with us tonight. On and on the Word sprang from me, a miraculous gift that seemed to unfold before my very eyes. I had no notes, but I had the Holy Spirit. I spoke of who the precious Holy Spirit is and it flowed out of me – the life that was inside of me spilled out.

When I finished preaching we called people forward who were sick. Ron came alongside me and together we ministered to the sick, just as we always did, but this time I was 'leading'. It was a beautiful time where God made Himself known to the people and to me too. I knew that if I opened my mouth, He would fill it (Psalm 81:10).

Afterwards, I looked around at the people, glowing in the familiar peace that came after prayer ministry. Some were getting ready to go home; some were preparing places to sleep under the trees.

'Do you see, Keir?' Ron asked me. 'Look around here at the fruit of the gospel. These are the harvest! This is the Word of God! It's exactly what you have been called into! Well done!'

I looked around and I was awestruck.

Ron smiled at me. 'This is the Kingdom.'

It was true. The fruit of the gospel of Jesus Christ is always people carrying around the truth. It didn't come from hearing Ron's words or my words but by the power of the Holy Spirit. Jesus Christ made Himself known and people received a measure of heaven on earth. The gospel promised the good news of Jesus Christ and it delivered.

Ron took a risk that night by giving me the microphone, letting me preach to all of God's people. He did it more and more as we worked together. In his mind, He was being obedient to God. God had made a way for me to preach and I jumped in and did it.

'Now faith is the substance of things hoped for, the evidence of things not seen.' (Hebrews 11:1). What Ron had faith for was not me preaching, it was the Kingdom harvest. He had faith that God would make Himself known when I took that microphone and He did. Ron taught me that it isn't about the messenger; but about the message.

For two years I ministered with Ron Kussmaul Ministries. This was during a time of great unrest and conflict in Zimbabwe. The pressure for whites to leave the country was always in the background of our daily lives. We felt it doubly, since people heard that we had been to America.

A couple of men stopped my children once on their way home from school. 'Is it true your father has US dollars in that house?' they asked.

They looked at each other and said, 'No, we don't have American dollars.'

'Are you sure?'

Jenni took Simon's hand and walked away. Later, when they came home, they asked me if it was true. I wondered who the scoundrels were who could have asked them. I considered such a question to be threatening and no one threatens my children and gets away with it.

Our telephone line was wiretapped and we had to be very careful with what we shared on the phone. I was especially careful not to let on when I was going away since I would be leaving Callie and the kids behind.

Most of our friends had left. We had ties to the land and it was my home as much as anyone else's. I would not be bullied or pressurized into making a decision but one evening a friend of mine took me aside and told me that our lives were in danger.

'Keir, I have it on good authority that you need to leave the country, and soon.'

I nodded, listening carefully. 'Do you?'

He was very discreet in telling me but he made it clear and I got the message. 'You can pack up a removals truck and leave with your belongings now, or we can hide you on a remote farm and you can live there for a while. The trouble with that is that you may have to flee in the middle of the night with no belongings.'

Callie and I talked and decided that we should pack up and leave as soon as we could. I had received an invitation to join the staff of a church called 'Fill the Gap Ministries in Johannesburg – a church that had a strong missions focus. I accepted and within a week we were packed up. On Easter weekend we left our homeland, driving a pick-up pulling a trailer of our belongings. I remember the sadness as we drove away with just a few belongings and our children (Callie also took her favorite dog – a little poodle named Muffy). By God's grace we were able to cross the border undetected and drove into South Africa.

The church had arranged for a rental house for our family - we drove straight to it. Johannesburg was everything it was reputed to be, a crowded city surrounded by gold mines and townships. By the time we reached the house, we were exhausted. I wish I could say that we drove up to a welcome party, to a safe house that would be our refuge… but we didn't. At the sight of the house my heart sank. The overgrown grass was touching the dilapidated windows; the paint was peeling. The inside was not so bad – but it was stark and bare.

Another house with no furniture? We had done this before, even with kids but I was didn't want to go through the whole thing all over again. Our own furniture was scheduled to arrive later in the week with the removals van. I had only three hundred Zimbabwean dollars in my pocket (the equivalent of three hundred South African Rand back then). There was no one there from the church to welcome us or even to explain the accommodation. Somehow we obtained the key from the letting agent and that night we slept on the floor on some blankets.

By some miracle, a family from the church found us the following day. They came to our door, introducing themselves as members of the church and explaining that they didn't know we had arrived. They were driving around the neighborhood, wondering to themselves: 'Do you think that family from Zimbabwe is going to live around here somewhere?' They saw our car; with Zimbabwe number plates and a trailer attached and put two and two together. Their knocking on our door was an act of faith.

We didn't have anything but that afternoon they rallied the church and began to bring things to us: cutlery, plates, things to eat, beds (so we would have somewhere to lay our heads) and essentials like soap and toothpaste. The outpouring of love was much appreciated and very humbling.

It was a very tense time in South Africa, the early 1990's. The apartheid era was coming to a close and the residents lived in a strange mixture of hope and dissatisfaction. The national language was still Afrikaans, which made it hard for us. We were English to the core, and as we tried to communicate with Afrikaans-speaking people everywhere, they would turn away and not answer us. In many ways it was a greater culture shock than moving to America.

While in Johannesburg I made my living as an itinerant pastor, travelling around the country talking about the value of missions and the importance of the Matthew 28 calling. I felt strangely dissatisfied with this job, especially since I wanted to go out and do it, rather than just talk about it.

———

It wasn't too long before God spoke to me about moving house again:

'Son, it's time for you to settle down and become part of a local church.'

'Really? I am, Lord. I'm part of a local church now.'

It was clear that He meant something different. 'No, not that one.'

I had been walking closely with God for a while, long enough to know that when God whispered in my ear, something was coming – I just didn't know what. Soon I was invited to Pinetown in the eastern part of South Africa to join the staff of a church called City of Life. Again, we packed up our belongings and went to Kwazulu Natal, to join the staff of another church. During this time, God's favor was on us. Through a variety of gifts and some careful saving, we were able to buy a house, one that Callie could build a lasting nest in. We put down roots in Pinetown and I've never regretted it.

There at City of Life, I was a local pastor, being used by God but very discontent to be staying in one place and not going out to evangelize at all. One evening in a church service, the pastor had a prophetic word for me: 'Keir, you are the square peg in the round hole!'

Without missing a beat, I yelled back at him: 'Why don't you send me out, then? I'm ready!'

I felt so misunderstood, so hungry to get back to the work I was doing with Ron. I wanted more than anything to be released into the evangelical calling that I felt so deeply in me.

One day God spoke to me:

'Get ready, son.'

Like a good son (and soldier) I was ready at a moment's notice, giddy with anticipation.

In a few days, Rod and Ellie Heine, some friends of ours who were living in South Africa (but knew us from Rhodesia) invited me to be part of a team going to Mozambique to meet with a group of church leaders. They had planned a massive church conference deep in the bush, in a remote location away from major cities and were assembling a team who could travel to meet them and minister to their needs. There were also going to be plenty of chances to minister into the nearby villages. Rod planned to fly us in - under the radar so that we could not be detected by the warring factions of RENAMO and FRELIMO. The whole idea of the mission excited me; I was in!

That morning we left with a four man team: Jaco, Mike (our future son-in-law) Jeremy and me. Mike and Jeremy took a vehicle in but

Jaco and I were flown into the remote location in Mozambique by Rod. We could see flocks of chickens taking cover as we were flying so low. We flew for about two hours until we approached a large clearing in the middle of nowhere. We landed on a crude airstrip and the plane taxied to a stop. Out of the bush, I could see a group of soldiers drive up on motorcycles, AK-47s strapped to their backs. Clouds of dust followed them; it was the dry season.

We jumped onto one of these motorcycles and followed them to where we would meet the leaders of the churches in the area. It was astounding to see them all gathered, seven hundred men and women who wanted nothing more than the presence of God and Biblical direction on how to build their churches. They had been lying down under the trees; resting anywhere they could lay their heads.

We set up our tents about fifty meters from where we were planning on teaching, an oddity to the villagers. They watched in fascination as we erected our camp. Not far from us was a water source where we could draw safe drinking water. After teaching in the morning, I decided we would take some of the leaders with us as we walked to the nearby villages. Nearby we were told that there was a clinic, so I decided we should start off there. We came to the 'clinic:' a shady tree with a grass mat on the bare earth and a clay pot of cool water. A little boy was lying on the mat; the nurse was sitting next to him on a rock, obviously feeling helpless and exhausted.

We approached him and the leaders looked at me. I knew of no formula to heal sickness other than the Word of God, so I opened to James 5:14 and read it aloud:

> *'Is anyone among you sick? Let him call for the elders of the church, and let them pray over him, anointing him with oil in the name of the Lord.'*

I took out a flask of oil from my knapsack and anointed the boy's head with it. 'Gentlemen, we're the elders here let's all lay hands on him and pray.' The boy was instantly covered with hands; the pastors began to call upon the name of the Lord and we joined our faith together. Afterwards, we nodded in agreement.

'Well,' I said. 'We've prayed the word, it's up to God to do His work and we can go on in faith, believing we've done all there is to do.'

We walked on to the first village, a small place with mud huts surrounded by cornfields. We called out to the occupants. Village life has its own protocol and the leaders must invite you in if you want a friendly reception. It turned out that the particular village we were visiting hadn't seen white people in about eighteen years, and those whites were definitely not friendly. With careful trust, the leaders welcomed us in - and in true Mozambican fashion - they made us feel like family. They set out their best chairs for us, served us tea and welcomed us to sit in the courtyard where the village elders met.

We exchanged pleasantries until I spoke up boldly, not wanting to waste time. 'We are here with a message from a King that is of eternal importance for everyone,' I began. 'This is the message – it is about one man whose name is Jesus.' I began to preach the gospel, which they listened to quietly and politely. Afterwards, I told them I could prove this man Jesus still lived and walked among us as we moved. 'Is there anyone here who is sick? We will pray for healing.'

Many people came to us to pray for them; many people were sick and instantly got better as we prayed. I had never seen people who were so receptive to healing- it was exciting! As we prayed, two of the leaders left us and went ahead to the next village (without my knowledge) to alert them that we were coming and performing miracles. In the meantime, the village we were in was exploding with joy and celebration – they agreed to join us for the training time. Salvation came upon them mightily that day!

We reluctantly left that place, knowing there was much work to be done and more villages to visit. Many of the villagers followed us, clapping and singing and celebrating. As we approached the next village, we could see from a distance approximately one hundred people waiting for us to come to them. As soon as they saw us, they were ecstatic, waving their hands in anticipation.

They were so excited and, since we were being followed by a group who had just been filled with the Holy Spirit and healed of all kinds of things themselves, it was easy to be joyful. I tried to say the same thing, tried to preach the gospel of Jesus with the same certainty but I couldn't help but be filled with new authority and joy. The explosion of grace showered the people of that village and as we left them, many followed us to the next village. Each time I preached, each time I prayed, each time I stepped forward that day it was with more anointing- more faith. By the time I got to the last village, we had about five hundred people following us, clapping, singing and celebrating.

The last village we approached was remarkably different. It only had two people in it. As we approached, they were sitting down and looked relatively unwelcoming. The couple, it turned out, were the local witchdoctors, or sangomas. They were dressed in traditional witch-doctor clothes, beaded headdresses and with bones surrounding them. Bits of cloth were hanging from trees. I greeted the man and shook his hand, an action that made our celebrating crowd go completely silent. In their culture, no one touched the witchdoctor.

'I am Keir,' I said to him. 'I have come to bring you and your wife the good news of Jesus Christ.' With the deafening silence of the crowd behind me I delivered the same message to these two that I had to every village I had visited that day. This time, the reception was no different. The woman ran into their hut and grabbed a bag – an animal skin stuffed with trinkets and dumped it on the ground. In it were treasures – British sovereign coins, gold pieces, silver coins and rings – a fortune. The woman and man had actually been 'praying for relief' earlier that day, to an unknown God, who as it turned out, brought them us!

Now, in true surrender, the woman dumped her treasures out, knowing that we would charge something to bring her the forgiveness and hope of the most high God. I refused it, and the couple was astounded. The gift of Christ – His most precious salvation - is free! The witch doctors, in complete repentance made a fire and threw in all of their muti. The crowd behind me watched as skins, skulls, yarns and ropes were tossed into the fire.

The couple was so humble and repentant – they seemed to understand that their old life was gone. Their old identity was now in that fire and their hope rested in the free gift of Jesus Christ.

That night we held our first meeting in that village. At the beginning, the place was completely crowded but when the newly converted witch doctors came, the place grew silent. All of the villagers knew who they were. People from every village had visited them at one time or another, offering whatever meagre possessions they had in the hope that they would get some magic answer to an insoluble problem. Now they were showing up at a church meeting? There was fear in their eyes, but soon they realized that the couple was not wearing their witch doctor gear. What was going on?

'Come up!' I shouted to the couple. 'Come and share the salvation of Christ with your neighbors!'

The couple came up to share what had happened. There was a mixture of joy, disbelief and celebration as they shared. The villagers were suspicious; was this a stunt? They also feared a loss of the safety net they had in this couple. After all, what if God's salvation wasn't enough? What if they needed the witchdoctor later?

'Friends,' I addressed this concern right away. 'God has brought salvation to this area today. This means He is enough for you from now on. From this day forward, there will be no need for the witchdoctor or for traditional magic in this area! Jesus Christ is both your Lord and King'

There was joy and celebration and we began our meeting, worshipping and dancing. I prayed that God would solidify this whole change. After all, we were leaving soon and what would happen afterwards would be up to God - and God alone.

On this trip I had to face something terrible that I was not prepared for.

The casualties of Mozambique's long and terrible civil war were all around us. That week there were two women wandering around in the bush, totally lost. They were emaciated from starvation and had no home or support. One of them was an old lady in her 70s, whose brown skin showed signs of dehydration and malnutrition. She was traveling with a young girl, possibly twelve years old. They were victims of the Mozambique war; their home had been burnt; their families had been tortured and killed. By some miracle, they had escaped and walked towards the conference.

I found out much later that the old woman had had a dream during the night before she came to the conference. In it, an angel had come to her and said 'Go towards the setting sun and there you shall find help.' For two days the ladies staggered through the bush in the hope of finding the promised help.

When they found the conference site, they rejoiced, thinking that this was the place of help that the angel spoke of. They were directed into the area where the coordinator was late one afternoon and pleaded for some water and a little food.

'Wait over there and you will be attended to,' the coordinator said.

The ladies wandered off to a small broken-down hut at the edge of the sprawl of huts. With fires and people milling about; they waited there until sunset.

Unaware of all of this, our team rested after the conference by our fire. We debriefed and finally went off to bed, basking in the glow of all that God was doing.

The following day, while I was busy teaching the leaders, my translator was suddenly interrupted. A young man came into the meeting and walked up to the platform, telling the translator something of importance in a low voice. When he left, the translator stood up straight and looked at me.

This kind of disruption happened in these conferences but I wanted to make sure all was well. I leaned a little closer to him and asked, 'Is everything alright?'

'Yes, it is,' he answered. 'Everything is good.'

At the end of the meeting I turned to my translator and asked what the interruption was about. Being in a hostile area with war lurking all around us, I needed to know. His face changed and he grew solemn.

'Someone died here last night,' he said.

I know that life and death are normal occurrences, but in the bush of Mozambique the funeral would most likely occur swiftly. I knew we should go and visit with the family and possibly attend the funeral. It was not uncommon for a conference like ours to come to an abrupt halt as the deceased is dealt with.

'May I see the immediate family?' I asked

The translator seemed to hesitate a bit but he agreed. I followed him out of the meeting area and into the surrounding fringe. Jaco came with me, as did other conference leaders.

We came to a shabbily thatched hut on the fringe of our compound. At the door sat an old woman, gazing out into a harvested cornfield. She did not move, but her eyes looked up at us as we went into the hut. There on the floor, covered only with a loincloth, lay the body of a young girl. She was curled up on a dry goatskin in a fetal position, with her hands clasped near her head. Instinctively I reached out my hand and touched her head; it was cold.

'Raise her from the dead!' a voice screamed inside me. I didn't even pray for resurrection, the fear and hatred of what had happened to the young girl was swirling inside of me.

I looked at the translator and then at Jaco.

'Where are her relatives? I asked.

I don't know' the translator replied.

'What was her name?'

'I don't know'

'Where did she come from?'

'I don't know, Keir.' Finally, the story came out: 'The woman and the girl had come in last night as we were getting ready for the conference. They were told to wait to the side and we planned to come back to them but when we looked around for them, they had gone. Later, we completely forgot about them. We were so busy …' His voice faded, and then he shook his head. 'I'm sorry.' A tear rolled down his cheek.

'What happens now?' I asked him.

He began to walk to the door, stopped outside and turned to face us both.

'I will take care of this burial,' he said. 'And her too.' He was indicating with his hand that the old lady outside was part of this. She had lost this child and was now grieving; where were the words to comfort her? We were responsible!

I felt a volcano rising up deep inside me. I turned and walked into the cornfield, no longer able to control my tears. I kicked everything in my path and lashed out at the dried-up stalks in front of me. I was white-hot with rage, frustration and helplessness.

'How could this happen? How could these coordinators think that the details and organization of this conference were more important than these women and their lives? Why? Why? WHY God did you let this happen?!'

By the time I calmed down, I was exhausted and covered in dust. I strolled up and down by the edge of the field and the encroaching bush. Eventually, I was quiet enough to hear His still, small voice.

'Now you know how I feel. Now you know how I have felt about this world for a very long time.' I breathed deeply. I began to understand with a depth that no man could ever explain, teach, or reveal to me. 'This is the same way my Son felt when he saw the multitudes,' The Spirit of God came upon me like the day in the Nyadzonya Raid. I fell to my knees as I heard Him say. 'Will you go where no others will?'

What else could I say? Could I refuse because of my broken heart? God's heart was greater than mine and He had to witness much more than I ever could. It was a deeper revelation and, therefore, a deeper calling than I had known before.

'Yes, Lord' I whispered, 'Lord, now I know.'

I remained there until sunset. Something deep inside of me had changed. There was no more anger and frustration; it was replaced by peace. I surrendered that day to a deep call that has never left me.

God had set me and, therefore, no man could ever upset me.

Every time I prayed for people, I felt a deep yearning to go deeper into Africa, specifically to Zambia and Mozambique. The desire seemed to be one that was planted by God, fanned into flame by the Holy Spirit. It grew larger every day.

I knew this would be no easy task. The roads into Mozambique were heavily guarded and the Tete run was controlled by a government escort - I would certainly not be welcomed. In any case, our family sedan (an old Toyota) would never make the trip on the rugged Mozambican roads. Until God gave me a four-wheel-drive that could handle bush terrain, I could not even entertain the idea of going in. Even if heaven opened up and dropped a four-wheel-drive in my lap, who would be my contact on the inside? I would need to find a man of peace on the inside, (Luke 10:5-6) one who had the same passion for spreading the Word of God.

One night I went to a prayer meeting with a friend. While I was there, a lady I had never met before came up to me with a slip of paper in her hand. 'This is the name of a man who will be an important contact for you,' she said. 'He will be a man who will open the doors of Mozambique for you.'

I remember feeling encouraged, as if God had heard the silent prayers of my heart. At the same time I felt stuck, logistically speaking. How was I to travel to Mozambique? I had done so before with Ron Kussmaul; I knew how rugged the roads were. I needed better equipment.

'Lord, you know all things. You know I need a four-wheel-drive, don't you?'

God simply whispered, 'Keir, what do you have in your hand now?' (Exodus 4:2)

I was out by the back of our home, near the garage. There in front of me was our Toyota sedan and my motorcycle, a Yamaha XT550.

'Do you mean the motorcycle?' I asked, incredulously. 'This? Callie would not be impressed at all!' I waited for Him to respond but no answer came. Instead, a slow realization dawned on me; this was what I had in my hand. Was this the vehicle that I would use to make the six hundred kilometer journey with two border crossings – navigating wildlife, cows, goats, rough roads, drought, war, and pestilence? The motorcycle could do it. It was also capable of crossing the border and would be stealthier than any other vehicle.

It was a risky move but anything was better than staying still. I made a decision to do it and set a date. I took the bike to a mechanic friend of mine and told him 'This motorcycle is going to take me to Maputo and back. Make sure it is as capable as possible.'

I readied myself for the journey by swimming two kilometers a day. I researched what gear I would need and questioned others who were used to making long motorcycle journeys. Of course I spent deep times in prayer and the Word.

I got on that bike with two things in mind: travel to Mozambique with the good news of Jesus Christ and meet the man of peace, Joab Zimbini.

The ride into Mozambique began before dawn: I was up early,

Pioneering into Africa: ministry on motorcycle.

knowing I would have to cross from South Africa, through Swaziland and into Mozambique before nightfall. It was a rough trek, to say the least. I had to dodge people and cars and trucks were not normally very considerate of motorbikes. I also negotiated the dusty roads of Mozambique, avoiding potholes and landmines in certain places. At one point, the road crossed a war-torn area where burnt wrecks and tanks lined the road.. When I got to Maputo, I saw the city streets were a mess – raw sewage had been running through the middle of town and I had to keep my mouth closed at all times, just in case an unexpected pothole caused it to splash up in my face.

I finally reached the spot where I met Joab Zimbini for the first time. It was the beachfront and the ocean with a setting sun was behind him. He greeted me warmly and I was grateful and relieved to be there but I was completely exhausted. He led me off to his house where he offered me accommodation.

I had done it! I'd made it to Maputo in eighteen hours.

The next morning Joab and I talked heart to heart. He was grateful beyond measure that I had come to help him.

'No one has ever offered to help us here,' he said. He wasn't looking for sympathy, only hope that a fruitful relationship could be built. 'I have prayed very hard for this day to come.'

He told me of his plight as a Christian pastor under the communist rule of Samora Machel. The country had been stripped of any religious freedom; public worship was abolished, those who attended church were considered imperialist sympathizers.

President Machel made no secret that the FRELIMO government was anti-Christian, he vowed publicly that the destruction of the Church in Mozambique would be done in his reign. Machel called the priests 'puppets' and 'manipulators' – Protestant Christian churches he hated even more.

With the President calling Christianity the 'remnant of colonialism and a tool of fascism', thousands of churches in Mozambique were closed -barred up, bolted, chained and padlocked, burned down.

'Some churches were kept open, but they were nothing more than places for FRELIMO to hold meetings,' Joab told me. 'Structures to manipulate people.'

Missionaries were expelled; some were imprisoned first. Evangelism was forbidden. Bibles were ceremonially burned and tens of thousands of Christians, including many pastors and elders, were prevented from preaching the gospel, many lost family members through the war.

I sat and listened, stunned. 'What about you?'

Joab smiled. 'I was in prison for a long time. My own congregation tipped the guards so that they wouldn't beat me.'

He described 'Sjambok' beatings of fellow pastors who were held prisoner alongside him. The razor-like cuts would sometimes not heal and the infection would kill or cripple the person.

'But now,' he said, smiling softly. 'Now you are here.'

'Yes,' I said.

'Tell us everything – God has sent you for such a time.'

For a week I sat with him and his team and other leaders of churches, sharing the Gospel of Jesus Christ. They were eager to hear all about the steps to salvation, the prayer of a repentant sinner. Physical healings and the power of the anointing were teachings they had never heard before. For almost two decades there had been no prayer ministry or calls for salvation. No one heard of Jesus Christ as both savior and healer. They had been 'informed' about a God but had no revelation of truth. The tradition of man had nullified the power of God.

I had the privilege during those days of showing them word for word in the Bible that He, Jesus, is the same yesterday, today and forever

At the end of one week, I was sent off by all of them; they were grateful and hopeful that I would return.

'And you will come back?' Joab asked me.

'Yes, I will come back,' I promised. It had cost five hundred South African rand for me to make the trip. It was a small fortune at the time but it meant the world to these men and to me. I had finally made the trip that would change my heart forever – a trip meeting the remnant of the church here.

My brothers in the faith – I am still in awe of them.

———

For three years I travelled in and out of Mozambique on that motorcycle. Joab introduced me to many leaders and eventually I began networking more and more into the country. I continued to go into many areas in the Gaza and Maputo regions. Now and then other guys would come with me; many more men expressed a desire to do the same. I started to build up teams that would come with me and do the work that I loved doing; the discipleship of the nations (Matthew 28:18-20) with the five-fold ministry (Ephesians 4:11).

Eventually, I had developed a whole strategy for putting a team of men together that could make the trip with me.

In the early days of the 1990's I decided to run an open-air power crusade where the gospel could be preached to thousands in a public place. I acquired a vehicle – a one-ton truck (not a 4x4) that some businessmen had bought for me and I was given a couple of loudspeakers and microphones. A generator was also given to me as well as some lights and a platform. After years of religious persecution, the people of Mozambique wanted to hear the gospel preached and the Word of God read. They wanted to worship with freedom and joy.

There was a bit of homework to be done before we could do a crusade. I had to meet with the local fraternity of church leaders to gain their permission and (hopefully) support. I also had to have the permission of the mayor or governing authorities. The police and security had to be satisfied that I was not staging a political rally. Once I had the legal permission, we would meet with the church leaders and strategize about how to put on a crusade.

On one occasion, I went to quite a bit of trouble to stage a crusade in the city of Chibuto in the province of Gaza. A team comprising Australians, Dutch, British and South Africans wanted to come with me to stage the event. I went up beforehand to meet with the mayor and fraternal leaders to get the proper permission to operate. I also made the necessary logistical arrangements (site, police, permits, etc.). Six weeks later I returned with a team of twenty-five people.

The first thing I did was set out to meet with the fraternity of churches to have their consensus. To my surprize, they were in disagreement. They asked me not to put on the crusade since they couldn't reach a consensus. It was disheartening. I had never had opposition from local churches before.

I went back to the mayor.

'What is your opinion and decision on this event?' I asked him. 'Do we still have your permission to put on this crusade?'

'Yes,' he said. He wasn't sure why I was asking. 'We've agreed on this and you should do what you came to do.'

'Well, I'm afraid I don't have the support of the local fraternity and it might not be wise to continue. I do not want to bring division to the local churches here in Chibuto'

The mayor seemed to be sympathetic, agreeing that it was discouraging that the leadership couldn't agree but he didn't see this as a hindrance. 'It's sad that the fraternal leaders aren't with you, but you must do what you came to do.' He handed me a letter with his stamp of approval on it. With that, we left his office and started to break ground.

In a dusty field we erected the equipment. Within minutes we had a crowd, watching and waiting to see what would happen. That evening we hosted a time of music and singing before the teaching. Before long we had a large crowd of people dancing freely in front of the platform. The first night of the crusade, there seemed to be a spiritual tension, as if we were being affected by the lack of unity amongst the community leaders.

The second night of the crusade was a blur of activity. I remember saying, 'There are three or four ladies here with cancer. The Lord wants to deliver you tonight!'

As I said this, three ladies came out from the crowd, two of them limping badly. Soon another one emerged, hunched over. They all looked very ill. As I placed my hands on one woman's back, I could feel the lumps of tumors all down her spine. The second woman had more of the same. I felt a holy anger rise up in my heart and I knew that this would be the turning point of this crusade. Through the translator I asked:

'Do you have faith for healing tonight?

'Yes!' they said without hesitation.

'Do you believe that Jesus is your healer?'

'Yes!' they said.

'Therefore according to your faith and belief in the words you have heard tonight and the authority that Jesus has given the church, I say cancer, you are cursed and evicted from these bodies in the authority and power of Jesus Christ!' I prayed with all my heart, cursing the very root of cancer. The third woman had the same thing in her neck – a large ball at the side sticking out and hard to the touch.

We all prayed and then went on with the crusade.

The third night of the crusade I returned to the site and saw that the crowd had grown bigger. There was music playing and on the platform were some ladies dancing. I turned to Jorge, our translator, and asked him, 'What's going on? Why are those women on the stage?'

'Those are the women from last night,' he said, happily.

'Which women from last night?' I was struggling to remember whether I had met them before. Jorge laughed.

'Those were the ladies with cancer. They have come up on the platform and they want to testify of God's faithfulness to heal them! Look at them now, they are busy celebrating!'

I was astounded – they didn't even look like the same women! I ran over to the platform and jumped up onto it and checked for myself to see if the tumors had, in fact, left their bodies. Sure enough the woman's spine was clean and straight. The other woman's neck was without any lump – I could not contain my joy!

'Stop the music!' I cried. 'These ladies came forward for prayer last night and now they are going to testify of their healing!'

The ladies shared their stories of healing with exuberance and great passion. The crowd broke out in thunderous applause and we all celebrated together – hundreds of people dancing and singing praise to the one great and powerful God. 'He is alive again in Mozambique!'

While the worship was going on, there was a man who came forward dressed in priestly robes. He was very solemn and as the crowd parted around him, I could tell he was respected. He came to the platform to where we were standing but I didn't recognize him as the leader of the fraternal union. At first I thought he might be there to rebuke me but then I could see that his face was sad. He knelt down in front of me. A hush fell over the celebration as he spoke: 'Please forgive me, brother,' he said in front of the crowd. 'I have seen what God has done here and what has happened in this town with this event. I know God is here among His people. I am wrong to have ever opposed this event and you. I ask for your forgiveness.'

I picked him up from his kneeling position, embraced him and assured him that I forgave him. 'Of course I do, but please never ever kneel before me! There is never any need to kneel before anyone but Jesus, is there?'

That particular crusade did not follow our pattern.

It lasted for three more days, with double sessions each night. The people would not leave, one of the local pastors started documenting the events that were happening because so many spontaneous healings occurred.

In the crowd I recognized two young men from a previous crusade we had done in Maputo a month before. I stopped in front of them and asked if they were pastors I had met before as they looked so familiar.

'We are the wide awake pastors,' they told me. 'Most of the pastors here are sleeping, but we are ready.'

I wondered what they meant by that but they explained themselves quickly. 'We come to the crusades you host and we plant a church for the people in that area. When we heard that you were here, we came right away. We are going to be planting a church after you leave. There are church plants in every other place you have been. We helped begin those church plants with the locals in that area!' They laughed and were gripping my hand, saying: 'God is building His church"

I smiled. God was indeed building His church there. Once the seed has been planted, a church's role is to water the Word of God, planted in those people's hearts. God is the one who brings the increase.

'Good for you,' I said. 'In six weeks we will be in Maputo again; I'll see you there!'

I traveled regularly with a faithful team of men who wanted nothing more than to see God glorified: Keith Abbott, Richard Olivier and (of course) our translator, Jorge. Once we were invited to meet up with a team of Americans who had set up a conference for the pastors of rural churches in Mozambique. At that time, it was a dangerous venture: Mozambique was in the throes of civil war and the conflict between RENAMO and FRELIMO severely restricted travel in and out of the country.

We made a plan to go in without military escort. We drove to the border of the country, rode our motorcycles to the Shire River, traveled in a dugout canoe to the other side and then hiked in to the meeting place with an armed guide.

Our guide was most likely a soldier who was picking up extra money; he carried a standard issue AK-47 and dressed in fatigues. Our hike was long and exhausting.

'How much further?' I asked him as it was becoming dark.

He lifted his arm and pointed towards a hill quite a distance from us. 'Just over that hill.'

We decided to make camp and sleep where we were as it was unwise to walk too far in the dark.

The next morning we carried on. When we came to the hill in the distance, we climbed up and over but still saw no camp.

'I thought you said it was here?' I asked him. He nodded and smiled.

'It is. Just over there.' He pointed to another hill, far in the distance. It took us another day of hiking over rough territory to reach the hill. When we climbed to the top of it, there was still nothing.

'If I ask you where it is,' I confronted our guide. 'You'll say it's not far, just over there, won't you?'

He smiled and nodded. 'Yes, it's just over there.'

Again, we made camp and again we rose early to hike another day. A three-day journey on foot in Mozambique is more strenuous than it sounds. There are the tall grasses, the threat of snakes and landmines, not to mention the thirst. We had not prepared ourselves for a three-day hike.

We finally arrived at the base; a large valley in the shade of huge acacia trees whose massive branches stretched out to provide a natural canopy; a place of peace. I could see why they chose this place. There was a small outcropping of huts and a water source. It seemed remote, perfect for a place to meet out of the eyes of RENAMO and FRELIMO satellites. We were the first ones there so we made ourselves at home. It took a whole day for the first of the American team to arrive. They had come on motorbikes and were quite surprised at the rustic surroundings. While they were friendly and happy to be there, they tried to hide their surprize that they would be staying in the huts that surrounded the base.

I couldn't help but smile; I knew they had no idea what they had gotten themselves into. That evening, we were told that our own accommodation was five kilometers away in a military base. We had even more hiking ahead of us before we could rest our heads.

The following morning I could see why we had come. Over two thousand leaders of bush churches assembled there under the acacia trees, thirsty to hear about God's design for building churches. There was incredible worship that began the conference; afterwards it was time for the teaching. The American team had decided to take first things first and begin with teaching about baptism. People were divided into language groups, under the massive Acacia trees. In our group a young man from the USA began to preach, telling the leaders the importance of baptism, how it's done and who should be baptized. It didn't take long for questions to arise.

'How many times should you baptize a person?' One man from the audience asked, raising his hand.

I knew the question arose from false teachings from the African Zionist Church. It was their tradition to dunk a person several times until they stopped resisting. As a result, many of these traditional pastors were taught that a person should be held under water until the inner demons left them so when the person stopped resisting, they were 'finished' being baptized. In reality, this practice was extremely dangerous. It was a good question and it was important that these leaders be taught the difference between baptizing and drowning someone.

The young man who was teaching (being American and, therefore, unfamiliar with the traditional superstitions) was nonplussed. He had a blank look on his face before answering.

'Just once.'

'Once?' Another man stood up. 'What about this Father, Son and Holy Spirit. That is three. Why not three times?'

The young man preaching was not used to being interrupted. It wasn't done in most churches, granted but these men were desperate for the truth.

'There is only one God,' he said. 'There is only one dunk underwater needed. It is a symbolic…'

'There are THREE dunks!' another man shouted.

There was a loud conversation between the pastors and soon there was a cacophony of argument in the crowd. The young man preaching realized that he was no longer in control of the meeting. Since the men were no longer listening, he had no choice but to leave the pulpit and sit to the side.

We decided to end the meeting for the time being. We retreated to have tea and the young man who preached sat down on a log, totally devastated. I felt bad for him, traveling the grueling journey only to be rejected by the local pastors. He was woefully unprepared for the crowd and I decided to try to encourage their team.

'The people you are addressing are leaders of churches,' I told them. 'Don't forget that they are leaders and trust us as leaders to bring the word of truth. There are certain African customs that these men are used to so the questions they asked the speaker were actually good questions. They only want honest answers from the Bible from us. Don't take it personally. Every culture has its own traditional beliefs that God challenges; this is just one of theirs.'

They seemed to understand my perspective and thanked me. They also agreed that they only knew the African traditions academically. Since I was familiar with their practices and all of the surrounding deceptions, I was the natural choice to teach about baptism in the next meeting.

I was delighted, humbled, and completely terrified. How could I follow this young man and bring order to chaos? There was only one way: the Word of God.

I stood up in the next meeting and began proclaiming the gospel of Jesus Christ. I used illustrations to highlight the triune (three-in-one) God: teacups, eggs, whatever I could get my hands on. I had the attention of the men; they could see exactly what we were talking about now. From then on, I told them that we were brothers – together in bringing God's truth to the nation – but that they were now responsible to bring the unadulterated truth of the gospel to this region. It would be up to them to express the importance of not mixing traditions or cultural interpretation with the Word of God.

When I had finished speaking, there was applause and I was relieved. Many of the pastors came up to thank me. At last they had solid answers they could point to in scripture. They were grateful that I understood their plight, living among people who had so many versions of the gospel. They were even more grateful that I didn't look down on them and treated them as absolute equals.

I didn't know what to say; all I could do was point to God. I couldn't help thinking that I knew what it was like to be them. I was once a student of the Bible being taught by foreign teachers who assumed I knew nothing. I knew what it was like to have my country judged as sub-standard and it was not fun. I couldn't help thinking that this was why I broke through that day. My experience shaped me into a better teacher; the tool that God needed to open their hearts.

———

On one of these trips, deep into the nation of Malawi I was standing alone by a trail, waiting for the others to join me. A man suddenly appeared out of the bush and started walking towards me. He was an old man, dressed in tattered clothes. Before he got close to me, I could tell that it had been a week or longer since he had bathed. I could also tell that he was coming to me for prayer.

As he approached I greeted him, extending my hand to shake his. He gave me the stubby remainder of what used to be his hand: a sweaty, slimy, twisted wrist with fingers that were displaced and pus-filled. It was all I could do not to withdraw my offer to shake hands; I swallowed hard and followed through.

He reached into his torn jacket and from his inside pocket he pulled out a yellow card, written across the top in big red letters was: LEPROSY.

I froze. I just shook the diseased hand of a leper- God help me! The man's eyes pleaded with me as he placed his hands together, simulating prayer. All this man wanted from me was prayer. I was moved with compassion and agreed. I placed my hand on the top of his bowed head and began to pray. When I did, the compassion of God came through me. It was as if heaven opened up and God's love went through me and into this man. I prayed, but to this day I can't remember the exact words I used. When I finished the man looked up at me, smiling.

His eyes were brown and round and wide; I looked into them and he seemed so thankful. He put the card back into his pocket and then, unceremoniously walked away.

I stood there speechless.

I remembered that in the Bible there were stories of Jesus touching lepers and healing them. The Bible wasn't overly descriptive, nor did it mention how horrific the advanced disease was. I had just come face to face with not only the disease, but also the person it held captive. I felt nothing but the love of God for this man, just as Jesus had for the lepers He prayed for. God showed me on that day that it is His compassion that heals people; more than the right words or the perfect prayer - His heart is to show love, even when those prayed for seem unlovely.

Sometimes, when we pray for people, it is more for our healing than theirs.

When someone tells me that they want the Kingdom of God, they very rarely know what they are asking for. Even Jesus says in Matthew 20:22 'You do not know what you are asking. Are you able to drink the cup that I am about to drink?' Of course his disciples said yes to him! They said, 'We are able,' but later they all deserted. Following Jesus and seeking after the Kingdom is a demanding calling with so much at stake. It requires a selfless subject to serve a magnificent King. There are seasons of giving and seasons of taking; always listening and always having faith that He is God – and you are not.

In Pinetown, we put down roots and I never regretted it. A family needs stability, especially with children. What I had hoped to share is that our stability didn't just come from our residence but from our faith in Jesus Christ. When I had children, I realized that I had only one chance to get it right. Callie and I tried our best to give the kids stability in both circumstance and belief and I could see that God had grace for us and allowed our children to feel loved and grounded. I am grateful to God that my kids are well-adjusted and wonderful human beings; they all love God and remain faithful in His service to this day.

People neglect their faith sometimes in the hope of building strong families, – which is a mistake. Faith is our shield, and this shield is only valuable if nothing can penetrate it. Kids need to be taught faith in God while knowing that they are not the centers of our universe. God is our hope and our purpose and our Lord. Our shield of faith requires that we, as people, pick it up and hold it closely to us according to the Word of God. This comes through time spent with God in His Word and in prayer; it is essential for us in our walk with God. All of the things that we learn are not isolated events, they are absolutely essential in order to bring the change that God wants to take place in a Christian's life.

Having been wounded, I learned a lot about the things that bring change. When a person is wounded in war, there is instant pain, fear that they may not be whole again and knowledge that there may be permanent disability. In many wars, soldiers who were wounded were taken back to a tent, stripped of their uniform and deprived of their buddies who knew them. The separation was sometimes worse than the wounds. They were treated as a number again, a bit of baggage in the way - of no use. Sometimes they returned home as a war vet; their identity was gone and they felt lost, their purpose, vision, manhood stripped from them. What was even worse was that no one could understand what they had been through. They left home whole and returned broken. Wounding brings an incomplete conclusion.

In Israel, during the Three Day War, the soldiers fought alongside the medics. They knew how to treat wounds in the field and medics there could even perform amputations. The Israeli army never took soldiers away from the field. They fought, bled and cried until that mission was over.

I thank God for Frank Robinson, the medic who fought alongside me and who was there to save my life at the Nyadzonya raid. He pulled me off the vehicle, checked my wounds, gave me morphine, bandaged me up, and put me in the vehicle next to him. I was valued and kept as part of the team; I was still a soldier. I still had camo cream on, I was not discarded as a hindrance to anyone, I was with them! I was embraced into the unit, not shipped back home like a useless nothing. That journey, as painful as it was, brought me a great sense of belonging.

Flesh wounds usually heal eventually; but a soul wound can linger for a lot longer. A lack of confidence can come as a result of the actual wounding process. Sometimes the confidence stays away for much longer than expected.

There is a sad joke that says, 'The Church is the only place that shoots its wounded.' Unfortunately, this is true to an alarming degree. Life dishes out things that wound us; we have to heal together, not alone. If we choose to adopt this principle of healing together, the church will be bulletproof. I don't want to be part of a people that discards its wounded; I want to be part of the church that has faith for healing while sticking together.

Church planting in remote areas.

Early days preaching open-air.

Preaching in Poland

On "the streets of no name"

Leadership training & conferences

Power evangelism in DRC

Passionately dedicated believers meet in outdoor venues in rural areas.

Mass meeting in Mozambique with several evangelists..

Leaders conference in Mozambique

A plane with Africa on it's heart

Keir Tayler

Our children, Lisa, Simon and Jenni

*Home church:
Cornerstone,
Pretoria,
South Africa*

*Keir & Caliie
Tayler, 2015*

AWAKENED AND STIRRED: THE HELMET AND SWORD

*...and take the helmet of salvation,
and the sword of the Spirit, which is the Word of God.*

Ephesians 6:17

Without a map (or a GPS) it would be impossible to get some-where you haven't been. Unless you've been there before, the route is a mystery. The Bible is the map (or GPS) to help us navigate life and its changes.

If it were not for the Bible, we could easily be led astray. If it were not for the Bible a 'man of God' might be able to tell you that a true Christian leader will stay in one place and shepherd a church. Another man of God might tell you that a true Christian leader should be able to teach complicated theology to the simple-minded. Still another might tell you that you can identify the man of God based on how he prophesies. If you spoke only to me, you might come away thinking that preaching the gospel in remote areas and planting churches was the most important challenge in our lives.

The Word of God clarifies this. It says that God gave all of these people to the church – some he made apostles (church planters and governmental leaders), others he made prophets, others he made evangelists. Still others he made pastors and then others he made teachers. In church we call this the fivefold ministry. Ephesians chapter four says that it takes all five types of leaders to have balance in the church here on earth. Why? 'For the equipping of the saints for the work of service, to the building up of the body of Christ.' (Ephesians 4:11, 12)

We are also charged in Proverbs 4 (vv 20-22) to

> *'not let (the Word of God) depart from your sight; Keep them in the midst of your heart; for they are life to those who find them and health to all their body.'*

With this strong exhortation in mind, we seek God with this map of life – the Living Word in our possession. Without it, we are lost.

———

Rodney Howard-Browne came to our church in Pinetown to visit and speak for three days. I'd seen him before and knew of his ministry, but when he came to us in 1998, things were different.

It is difficult to describe a Holy Spirit revival in words - they usually can't contain what God has done or is continuing to do. Suffice it to say that when Howard-Browne came, God poured out a river of anointing through him. I experienced such a new and beautiful touch of the Holy Spirit that I didn't want to leave. People in Pinetown and surrounding areas (even the unbelievers) choked the roads coming to our church, to hear and see this God who was making Himself known. The most incredible worship broke out; meaningful worship that fell on us like rain; came out of us like love. We sang hymns; had dreams awakened in us - we adored Christ together.

Each night that Rodney Howard-Browne spoke, I was in the front row. Being a pastor in the church has its privileges and front-row seats are just one of them! Each time he asked if anyone wanted the ministry of the Holy Spirit, I went forward. I didn't care how I appeared to anyone; I wasn't there to minister to anyone, I was there to receive! I knew the anointing when I saw it and I wanted more. This went on for six weeks; eventually the season came to an end.

Not long after this time, Callie and I took the kids to Zimbabwe to go for a holiday. We visited her mother and a lot of our friends. One evening we visited a couple and were invited to share and teach at their home group.

We decided to share about the anointing of the Holy Spirit and the meeting went on for hours. A powerful anointing broke out again and the people there drank it in. After the meeting that night, others came over the following day. There were continuous meetings at our friends' home while we were there. By the time we left (our favorite vacation) their small home group had grown to sixty people, enough to start a church.

As much (or as little) as I know about God, I do know that He delights in pouring out the anointing. I don't think it's wrong to dwell in His anointed places; it is what heals us and makes us contagious to others – even unbelievers.

I delight in the presence of God, in the anointing of the Holy Spirit. When it is genuine, it cannot be copied nor can it be denied. It brings a deep healing when you stand in the presence; heals us down to the core. It is the best thing there is on this earth and anywhere else.

His presence is worth any sacrifice.

In Pinetown, God solidified the calling on my life. Not only was I the happiest when I was functioning as an evangelist, God seemed to be using me the most when I functioned this way. It was the most amazing, beautiful time. I realized that God took great delight in using me as an evangelist – I became a weapon in His hand.

We were part of a local church but realized that the work we were doing in Africa could not be supported solely by our local church. Callie and I decided to start an NGO (a non-governmental organization, or non-profit group) that we called Hand in Hand International. The thought of us taking hold of the Hand of God and allowing Him to lead us as we followed was the inspiration for the name. That was how we lived; how we believed - God was our Father/leader and our hand was in His.

We registered with the South African government, but we never broadcast or promoted Hand in Hand publicly. Since it was tax exempt, we registered our vehicles under Hand in Hand and took care of necessary expenses for the trips through its funds. For the crusades, we were now transporting generators, sound systems, lighting systems and a team of people who knew how to operate all of these things. The expense was great, but so was the interest to support it. Many of our friends in America wanted to support the work we were doing; it was my delight to direct them to the NGO when they asked us about giving to the ministry.

Far from being a para-church organization, Callie and I saw Hand in Hand as the helpmate of the church, not the replacement for it. Whenever I ministered into a place, I was sent by my local church;

when I went I ministered into a local church, or with the cooperation of the local churches. God reaches the lost through the local church and also provides a home for the displaced and lonely. Our local church was our family, the safe place we called home with people who loved us. God's plan for building His Kingdom has always been – and will always be- the local churches.

The more I went out, the more I saw how necessary all the gifts of the fivefold ministries are, how closely they function together and how dependent they are on one another. I understood (with great passion) how to function in my own calling as an evangelist but as I went out, I increasingly understood and operated in the prophetic and teaching gifts. I understood the importance of the pastoral ministry, even if I didn't feel particularly comfortable functioning in that role. The apostolic calling, however, seemed to be the most misunderstood part of the fivefold ministry; something I had never given myself permission to function in.

After we started Hand in Hand International, things picked up speed. I was able to travel freely (with faithful teams) and develop lasting relationships with several churches in South Africa, Zimbabwe, Mozambique, Zambia and Malawi. These church leaders would want face time with me, many times asking how to find Biblically grounded answers to questions that were specific to their churches.

'I have three wives,' one pastor would share in deep humility. 'I know the Bible says I'm only to have one, but they depend on my support and to divorce them would not be right. They would be left without a place to live. What should I do?'

In another area, a pastor might ask: 'The Bible says it is a good thing for a man to aspire to be an elder. How do you tell the difference between a man seeking power and a man desiring to fulfill a calling?'

Still others: 'Does our church really need to give to the poor? We are already poor.'

'How often should someone be baptized?'

'Is there a way to lose salvation once it is attained?'

Depending on the area and the education of the local pastor, the questions would vary greatly. I considered carefully the relationship I had with each pastor. After all, I was more than a Bible encyclopedia; I was a trusted leader who they counted on to lead them in the truth.

Their questions were foundational and doctrinal so I never involved my opinion. Each time I gave direction, I showed them where in the Bible it was and for that they were grateful.

I realized that I was functioning in apostolic ways to these men. God was using me to encourage them in their calling; training them to find Biblical answers. It was my deepest desire that the leaders be counted worthy of the high calling of pastoring God's church (2 Thess. 1:11). I also encouraged training for church planting, especially among those who didn't have much. Whenever possible, I would provide a Bible to a needy pastor and tell him to study it with all his might.

Was this the apostolic? Had God really chosen me to give to His church in this way?

Back home, at City of Life, I was a pastor. It didn't seem to be my calling; I felt like a square peg in a round hole. There was no excitement in it for me and I always seemed to be inviting others to join in the fun of what we were doing in Mozambique.

It was during this time that I met Dudley Daniel, who led a team of men who functioned apostolically in South Africa and other parts of the world. I had heard about this team, who championed the fivefold ministry of Ephesians 4 to reach nations. Jenni and Simon were in high school about the time I met him, which was really just in passing at a church conference. He seemed like a nice guy and we talked a bit. I told him I was on my way to the USA to see friends and visit people who were interested in the work we were doing.

Dudley suggested that while we were in California we should meet with him and a group of leaders over there. He invited us to be part of a leadership training time in Los Angeles, California and I accepted. The next month, there I was at a church in the Los Angeles area with a group of Americans who were all wanting to take part in the same thing: building God's church on earth in every nation.

It was a very exciting leadership training that lasted for a week – they referred to it as a Trans-local Training Time. Dudley preached on the New Testament model of Church and the fivefold ministry (especially the apostolic). He explained the difference between those who functioned as local pastors or elders and those who travel 'trans-locally' to churches who invite them in to minister. It was crystal clear that this pattern is in the Bible and he taught it with the love and grace of God. Callie and I caught ourselves glancing at each other and nodding every other second. It wasn't just the message, or even the words he was using, Dudley seemed to have known us for years and was describing what was already in our hearts.

At the end of one of the sessions, Dudley sought us out and asked to have lunch with us. It was amazing; I couldn't wait to chat with him about all of this.

'Dudley,' I asked boldly. 'Where do I sign to be a part of this whole vision?'

Dudley smiled across the table at me. 'There is nothing to sign, Keir. There's not even membership in what we're doing.'

'But that's not the way it works, Dudley,' I said. 'In missions' organizations you sign up, then you are interviewed and maybe accepted or endorsed. After that there is partnership or cooperation with them.' I had had a variety of experiences with mission organizations, so I knew the ropes.

'Dudley looked me square in the eye and said, 'No membership, really. There is none of that. If you agree with what I've been talking about here, let's just shake hands and agree to walk together.'

'If this is true,' I leaned forward. 'Then heaven must be right behind you because I've never heard of this.'

The fact that there would be no hierarchy sounded like the best news I'd heard so far. New Covenant Ministries International (NCMI) sounded like a group that was doing what I was already doing, just in different places. Dudley understood the heart of God's design for the church and he seemed to value and express gratitude for what God had put into me.

At the end of that week (the Trans-local Training Time) one of the speakers handed out blank sheets of paper to those of us in the audience. He said, simply: 'Here's a blank sheet of paper. Write down what you thought of this week.'

I was the first one finished. I wrote: 'Where can I serve? Keir and Callie Tayler.' I handed it in and walked out of there.

We had never been to any of the other meetings that NCMI had for leaders in South Africa. In its embryonic stages, the NCMI leaders met in the Drakensburg every year to discuss ideas and strategies for church planting, New Testament building, leaders' training, etc. Also, the 'relating' churches were invited to celebrate together at the Bloemfontein conference in the heart of the Free State every year. Callie and I had never been; we were way too busy to get involved in another conference.

When I got home from L.A., I found a fax from Dudley, inviting me to a Leaders' time together to be held in Durban North at the Church of the Good Shepherd. Callie and I decided to attend. It was a decision that would greatly affect the next years of our lives.

When we arrived I saw many pastor friends who I knew from other churches. When I saw them, I asked, 'Hey, are you a part of this?' They'd smile and say yes.

Everywhere I looked there were pastors and elders of churches, missionaries and evangelists. Their being together would never have happened in any denominational conference, so I knew that this was different. Maybe it was as Dudley said: a handshake and a natural relationship.

Callie and I took a couple of seats and listened to Dudley's talk. As was the case when we were in LA, our spirits witnessed to the truth of what he was saying. At the end he called for the 'Apostolic Team' to come up – he even called Callie and me by name. We came up to the front and he introduced us. I hadn't done a thing for this organization (hadn't flown the flag, raised money for them or anything) but there we were at the front being introduced as leaders with them.

The next thing I knew, someone was coming forward to lay hands on us. A group of people lovingly laid hands on us and prayed that God would continue the calling He had on us to disciple the nations. It was incredible; I was grateful for the prayer and when it was over, we sat down.

In Dudley's mind, he didn't need to 'make us leaders' in NCMI – we already were leaders. We were already 'functioning apostolically' and now we were in relationship with a group of those also doing the same thing, only differently.

We were invited to the Bloemfontein conference, which we attended the following week. Everywhere we saw people on fire for God, the same joyous worship broke out. The churches that met there were not cookie cutter churches that all looked the same; they were different expressions with different looking people. The more we spoke to leaders, the more we realized that there wasn't a 'be like us' mentality. The groups of people were different parts of the Kingdom – the gifts were all being brought together to create the joy that we saw: the church together and happy.

Towards the end of the conference, the same thing happened. Dudley came to the front and said: 'We want to introduce to you the new members of our apostolic team; many others and then - Keir and Callie Tayler.' There was applause and we started to go up, but again I didn't know why.

A guy was behind me and I turned to him and said 'Hey, what is going on?'

He smiled and said, 'Don't worry, Keir. Just enjoy the ride. You will discover as you go'

That's what it's been: a wild ride. The years we've had with NCMI have been an incredible ride, giving us support, encouragement and a pool of faithful people to work with. It has been an incredible time to drink in what we are really called to- building up the church.

I think the thing I love the most about belonging to our group of friends in NCMI is that I am affirmed in my calling. In the Kingdom of God there is no such thing as a square peg in a round hole. God makes square holes for us square pegs to fit through easily – and He delights in us.

As we got used to connecting with what we called an apostolic team, Callie and I received more invitations to come out and minister all over the world. Some friends of ours were based in Holland and invited us to come to them for a training time they were hosting. We went and were invited to share about God's transforming power to heal through His grace. It was a wonderful time; we met so many people there who asked us to come and minister the same thing to them all over the world.

One weekend in Holland, I met an Indonesian man who pastored a church and was filled with light and hope in Jesus. Right away, I knew we had a future working together.

'Keir,' he told me. 'I have friends who are leaders in churches in Poland who are dying for this message to be preached. They are desperate for some input and the healing touch of God! Do you think you'd be able to visit them and encourage them?'

'Well,' I answered. 'If you will arrange a meeting with more than one leader, I promise I will do all in my power to go there.'

With some careful planning, the trip was arranged and the following year we went. We arrived at the Rzeszów airport and I was introduced to this complicated land with its complicated language. The local leaders there had set up a conference and we had agreed to attend and minister. There were about twenty pastors and I had the pleasure of addressing them for about a day and a half.

The leaders there were (as my Indonesian friend had told me) excited about the visit. I shared a lot from the book of Acts and they drank in the truths of the gospel.

'We need the Holy Spirit,' they kept saying. I knew it was true; but in a different way than they were expecting.

'What you need,' I said boldly. 'Is a Spirit-led church; not a gift-dependent church.' I explained the difference – seeking God's face and direction is very different from the emotional explosions that most evangelical pastors are selling - or chasing. The Holy Spirit needs to lead and move, so we invited Him in and it was amazing

The power of God came and I laid hands on quite a lot of people. One of them was a pastor named Tomasz Manko. His church was in a city in the East of Poland, Radzyń Podlaski and we were invited to come and minister there. We did and the same thing happened. Desperate pastors and leaders longed for the Holy Spirit, all of them so wanting a touch of God.

As we left, Tomasz invited us to come back and minister again the following year. As we made arrangements to do so, God actually blessed us with a translator from Cornerstone church in Johannesburg – a woman named Natalia who was fluent in the Polish language. We were elated!

When we arrived in Radzyń Podlaski, Tomasz asked us if we would mind accompanying him to the house of a lady who had specifically invited us for morning tea. Callie and I were ready to withdraw and rest (we were still quite jet-lagged) but we agreed and made our way there with Natalia.

We drove across town to a row of communist apartment buildings-tall structures that were erected in the 1950s and 60s after communism condemned 'the excesses' of past decades. The apartments had no elevator and the woman's apartment was on the fifth floor with some very steep stairs. Normally, I wouldn't even mention this, but I was so tired- emotionally and physically- that I felt every single step of that walk up.

On the fifth floor landing stood a woman dressed elegantly in black, waiting for us. She greeted the pastor with enthusiasm but asked who I was. I could tell she was expecting a 'priest from Africa' – even in Poland they think that all Africans are black. I was also dressed in trousers and a shirt – not long, flowing robes.

We were welcomed into her apartment, a small but beautifully decorated place. The tea and coffee had been laid out as well as a magnificent looking chocolate cake. We sat down and visited for a while, exchanging pleasantries. The woman's name was Ewa and she had a young son, who sat politely on the couch as we talked. Within a few minutes the woman's daughter came into the room in a wheelchair, her name was Gosha and she was about eighteen-years-old. The girl had never been able to walk and only had mobility in a wheelchair; it didn't take long to realize that the flights of stairs kept her as a prisoner in her apartment, unable ever to see the light of day.

Natalia was able to translate what the mother was saying: the girl had a brain tumor, one so large and life-threatening that the doctor's had had to remove it. They operated on her several times and had actually removed part of Gosha's skull; they left a metal plate to protect the back of her head. The mother brought out a box-file of medical reports – doctors' reports and failed cures that the family had spent all their money on.

'This box-file,' the woman told Natalia. 'is a record of what medicine has tried to do to help, but it is limited and we are exhausted'. One thing that we didn't know was that in the kitchen was the father, listening to our conversation but refusing to be part of the meeting. He was so ashamed that he had no more money to take care of Gosha; he had no more money to see another doctor who may or may not be able to make her life better. Instead of anger, which the mother felt, the father only felt shame and failure as a father and provider.

After a while I asked Natalia if I could address Gosha. She agreed and

I spoke.

'Gosha, what if we pray for you today and the Lord does not heal you. What would your response be towards the Lord?'

Gosha was bright eyed. 'It doesn't matter. I have made up my mind that God is everything to me. He is the reason I am alive and the reason I am happy. The most important thing I have is my relationship with God, whether I walk or not.'

I was absolutely delighted with the response. 'I'm glad to hear you say that Gosha, that is a very mature response. Now I have a new question for you: What would you do if we prayed for you today and God does heal you?'

Again, Gosha was bright eyed and joyful. 'If God heals me today, I will take that box-file,' she pointed to the box of medical papers that her mother had showed us. 'And I will go and tell people, 'Here is what medicine can do for you,' and then I will walk in front of them. 'and here is what God will do for you."

I smiled broadly. 'Gosha, I am sure that this will please God if you do this; I'm also sure it will bless the church. I know you've been ready for God not to heal you but you also need to make yourself ready for God to heal you. After we pray, I'm going to ask you to do what only God can do; I'm going to ask you to walk.'

She smiled, 'I believe that.'

My heart leapt with expectation; we all stood around her and prayed. I lifted her footrests in readiness for her to put her feet down and walk. I moved furniture out of the way so that she would have a clear path to walk. We began praying together and I felt the palms of my hand become white hot. I remembered the verse in Habakkuk where it says that 'His radiance is like sunlight; beams of light shine from his hand, where his strength lays hidden.' (Habakkuk 3:4 ISV). The thought excited me and it was easier to have faith for healing.

As we finished praying, I waited. God was still doing something. When the warmth in my hands subsided, I took them away and looked at Gosha.

'Gosha, get up and walk to your mother.'

She leaned forward in her wheelchair, put her hands down on the armrests and lifted herself up. As she stood up, she was hunched over, still retaining the shape of her wheelchair. But she carefully started walking to her mother. The reaction in the room was amazing; the brother, who had been sitting on the couch collapsed in tears and wailed in disbelief. The mother clasped both hands to her mouth and wept -but was afraid to move because her daughter was walking to her for the first time in her life. Gosha was laughing and crying as she walked to her mother. Suddenly, the kitchen door shot open and in came the father, staring in disbelief. When he saw what was going on he began to weep uncontrollably, lifting his hands toward heaven. When Gosha reached her mother they embraced – laughing and crying. We were all in awe…

When everyone calmed down a little bit (and I mean a little bit – there was much rejoicing in that apartment!) I asked Gosha to walk back to her wheelchair.

'Push that thing away,' I said. 'Let it be in the corner of your room because you will spend the rest of today walking. When you greet other people you will lift your head high and be able to look them in the eye.'

It took a while but Gosha pushed the wheelchair back. We eventually left that apartment, all of them rejoicing and weeping.

The next day at church the mother came in carrying the file. At the beginning of the service, the mother testified. 'Look at this!' she said. 'This is what medicine can do! Now this is what God can do. Gosha, stand up!'

Gosha rose and walked forward to the stunned amazement of the church. What happened in the apartment the day before now happened at the church! There was celebration and laughter and weeping. It was the happiest time, filled with delight and joy in God's miracle.

The news of this healing spread everywhere through Eastern Europe. A television station wanted to come in and do a whole story about it, recording her testimony with the box of papers. Callie and I returned home, happy that God had made his healing power known in Poland. Apparently, this kind of thing didn't happen often there…

The next year I went back to Holland. I was talking with some local pastors, who reported that their faith had been stirred by many local miracles happening as God healed the sick all around them. One of them began to tell me Gosha's story.

'You know,' he said. last year this girl who had been in a wheelchair her whole life was healed and is now able to stand up by herself and walk. Apparently, some guy prayed for her and she just stood up and walked to her mother. Of course her mother was in disbelief at first, but the disbelief turned to joy!'

I smiled. 'Of course.'

'Yes, pastor! Isn't it amazing that God is still healing people out of wheelchairs?'

I nodded, beaming with joy. 'He is, He's amazing! He is the same yesterday, today and forever!'

With the move of the apostolic anointing came the season where Callie and I travelled extensively around the world. We were invited to many places in Europe, the Americas, Asia and Australia. We were asked to minister to leaders in the area of evangelism and the power gifts of the Holy Spirit. This stirred the pastor/teachers in these local churches to go out and do it! It was a wonderful time, albeit a bit exhausting.

I realized during this season that going out and functioning in the calling of an evangelist was still what made me the happiest. It was still the calling over my life. Sure, Callie and I functioned in the prophetic and apostolic, but I was Keir – the one who God called to be an evangelist. (Matthew 28:19, 20)

When we put our heads together and prayed, Callie and I came up with a plan: we could build teams of guys who were stirred to put their teaching gifts to work in other nations and take them into places that desperately needed (and were asking for) input.

We had moved to Pretoria a week after our youngest daughter, Lisa, was married and joined a church called Capital City Church, International. They had a lot of young leaders wanting to go into different parts of Africa, ready and able to spread the gospel.

I decided to make my first trip one that would establish our reputation as being a rugged team. There was an area in Mozambique near the towns of Mapai and Massangena - an arid region of people with a tragic history. They had been targeted many times during war, simply because of their position near a railroad. My heart broke for the people, who simply wanted a life for their children that was better than the one they grew up with. I wanted to be part of that new life; I wanted to help these villages in the best way that I could.

I plotted a course into the area through the Pafuri gate of the Kruger National Park. Since the roads would have to cross the Limpopo River when it was at a low level, it was necessary for all of the team to have 4x4 vehicles. The team soon formed – 25 to 30 guys who would convoy into Mapai in 4x4 s with some on motorcycles.

After spending two nights in Punda Maria (a campsite in the Kruger National Park) to train the team and check our equipment, we finally arrived in Mapai in the late afternoon. Since we had no established contacts with the local churches there, I endeavored to show the team how it was done. I found the first open place of business – a bar. I walked into the bar and said, unceremoniously: 'Does anyone here speak English?'

Everyone looked at me (even my own team). Suddenly, a guy stumbled toward us, eyes bloodshot and reeking of beer. 'I do,' he said over his heavy eyelids.

'Good,' I said. 'Can you take me to your town's mayor or a town clerk?'

The man stumbled outside and led us down the road and into a yard. There stood a man who was absolutely sober and tending to something in his garden. He bolted upright at the intrusion; I'm sure he thought he was going to be robbed by this drunken man. He was not impressed.

'This man needs to talk to you,' the drunken man stammered. The mayor looked past him and at me, wondering why I had chosen this late hour to visit.

'Yes? How can I help you?' He put down the tool in his hand and walked over to me.

I introduced myself and the team behind me. I then told him that we were there for an outreach – to build a bridge for future relationships for the gospel of Jesus Christ. I told him that I had never been there but had heard of the town. The mayor seemed receptive and asked me what I needed from him at that moment. I told him that I needed a meeting with the town leaders the following day and a place to stay.

'Until then, we need to find a place to set up camp. We need water and toilets and a place we can set up for twenty-five men. Can you suggest anywhere for us to set up camp without being a bother to the town or its residents?'

The mayor nodded. 'Follow this man,' he pointed to our drunken friend. 'He will take you to the fraternal leader who will show you where you can set up. Maybe he will let you camp at that place.'

I thanked him and shook his hand. We made an appointment to meet the following day to discuss the outreach.

The men followed me as I followed our tipsy translator to the fraternal leader. There was a large church ground where he allowed us to set up and use the toilets and water. Somehow we scratched together dinner that night. We prayed and thanked God for His faithfulness in getting us there

The next morning we met with the mayor as he had promised. In addition, he had also brought the Minister of Education, the military and the clinic staff. The fraternal leader (the director of all church happenings in the area) also joined us.

I thanked them for their hospitality and told them we appreciated their welcome since we had never been there before. We explained that we wanted to minister the gospel but had no church affiliation. We also told them we had teams that would put on dramas, minister music and prayer and we would also like to hold a crusade and welcome the people in surrounding villages.

In unanimous agreement, the men welcomed us, agreeing that they had been asking God for exactly this.

'For this reason,' the mayor said. 'This city is yours.'

It was a gracious reception and the guys could see how important it was that we connected with the village leaders and treated them with the honor they deserved. Many times, reckless evangelicals will come into an area, thinking they are bringing the blessing of the gospel but in the end only insulting village leadership. It was good that the men got to see the right pattern.

There was the beauty of bringing the gospel and ministering to villages, as always. There was also the wonder of new salvations. But, there was also the freshness of building up new leaders and I took delight in watching them function in their own callings. Some of the men were born to do it. Some of them needed more structure in the days we were there and weren't afraid to say so.

'Why are you so disorganized?' One of them asked me, completely frustrated. 'Don't you know what you're doing? You tell us one thing in the morning and then we end up doing another at the end of the day! Don't you have a plan?'

I wasn't really insulted or threatened; it was just a sign that this man was not cut out for the type of outreach trip that happened with me leading.

'My friend, when you are out in the bush this is how things go some-times. Do you think this is church?' I asked him. 'Start at quarter to ten, sing three songs, speak in tongues, read a poem, take up the offering with a special song item, listen to a three-point preach and then go home?' I shook my head. 'We are tearing up ground here! We are at war in the heavenly places. If you're not comfortable with hearing the wind of the Spirit blowing in the trees, maybe this isn't the kind of travel for you.' Then I would gently lead him to understand the whisperings of God and to be ready to follow God. After all, 'the mind of man plans his way, But the LORD directs his steps.' (Proverbs 16:9)

A few of those guys didn't come back again. It's not for everyone-pioneering into the bush requires you to be flexible and to live on the edge. It is exceptional training for surrendered people who want everything God has for them. Opening up new territories for the Kingdom of God is for the wild ones!

When you're out there, you have to be ready, humble, and teachable. Seeing God move in people and watching the gospel spread, being a part of it.

———

Callie and I visit churches that invite us and we have always been welcomed by the people. The church elders invite us to minister and we are delighted to. When we go and stay four or five days with people in one place, they catch what we carry in our hearts. It's not necessarily that they are impressed with our teaching but if we have the contagious Holy Spirit, they catch it. We always go into a church and endeavor to bring revival, divine healing, and salvation.

One of the jobs of an evangelist is to stir churches into revival so that evangelism will flow from it. Simply put, revival within the church will cause evangelism from the church; when you've got the fire you become fearless.

We were once invited to minister in a South African church that was in a mining community. They advertised that we were going to be there and we came, carrying what we held dear and precious in the gifts. The first night we were there we had worship, which led to words of knowledge and then to deaf ears being healed. There was so much joy as the Holy Spirit moved, mightily!

The second night we began the meeting and more people were there. The same giftings broke out and many came forward for healing. It was amazing! The next night, word spread through the community and many new people came in from surrounding areas for ministry. That night, the pastor approached me during worship.

'Keir, who are all of these people?' he asked me, incredulously. 'I've never seen them before!'

I asked if he was networking with them on Facebook or twitter. He didn't seem to know what I was talking about. I smiled and told him, 'Do you see that your church is evangelizing? They have loved the meetings and now they are inviting their friends and neighbors to come and meet God here!'

The pastor looked around and realized it was true. The pastor could see that once the gift was awakened in his people, the result was a church filled with new people! He began to dance and sing in worship – praising God for all He had done. The dreams for his church growing were coming true. It happened only because God was there and where He is there is life.

Imagine someone coming to your home and saying to you: 'Hi! Can I come in? I've brought you some gifts- here they are! They are revival, divine healing, and salvation!

What would you say? 'No, actually, now is not a good time. Go away, come back later?' Hopefully you would pull them in and say, 'Give me those gifts!'

These gifts awaken and stir people, even unbelievers! Why does the church not come out and say, 'Here are your gifts! Come and get them!'

When Callie and I were beginning our time in ministry, Dick Mills spoke a prophecy over us. He said: 'You will be sent to awaken churches, you must not fear, you will go with the power of the Spirit. You are not being called into 'the ministry… the ministry…the ministry.' You are being called to awaken and stir the church and its leaders. They may know My word but they don't know Me…."

Time after time this word has been spoken over us. Each time we are humbled by this word over our lives. We are stirred by it ourselves.

Salvation and its power are stirring. Divine healing shakes people – villages and cities alike! Revival causes hurricanes of change as it blows into town. These gifts are ours to receive. Come in, Holy Spirit! Give me those gifts – You are welcome in my house!

Keir and Heidi Baker, planning relief for the year 2000 Mozambique floods

7

ABSOLUTE PRAYER

'With all prayer and petition pray at all times in the Spirit, and with this in view, be on the alert with all perseverance and petition for all the saints'.

Ephesians 6:18

I wanted to put on a crusade in Bulawayo, so I travelled to Zimbabwe a week in advance with a friend, Keith, who faithfully ran the lights and soundboard. Keith and I stayed in a humble cottage not far from the center of town.

During those times in Zimbabwe, it was very tense politically and the people suffered tragically. The grocery stores had little to offer – sometimes only cleaning agents. People were forming queues for bread or bananas or anything they could eat. The scarcity of food was criminal; many times people would go days without nourishment and languished in the road, weak from hunger.

Keith and I had quite a lot of free time during the day. The cottage was big enough for us both to have some privacy, so most of my days were spent reading and praying. It was a season where I began to push in to the presence of God. I read several books on the presence of God. I intentionally studied the gifts of the Holy Spirit and read testimonies of God's divine healing. The words came alive and I felt like I was being given years of experience from their pages.

One day as I was reading I began to shake uncontrollably. It was so powerful that I had to get on my hands and knees and crawl to the bed. As soon as I did, I cried and shook and felt completely overwhelmed by the power of God. Eventually it stopped and I felt incredible peace.

I took this with me to the meeting that night. I saw things clearly there; I had words of knowledge for people that were very accurate – unusually accurate.

'You!' I pointed to a man to tell him what I saw for him. 'I see you in a big project, you've been building a house. I see it there, next to a big rock and a tree. You've got the walls built – you had a window here and a door there. I see your wife and children around you, getting ready to move in. Then as you built it, somehow it was taken from you. You are now here in Bulawayo and your whole self-worth and value has been stripped from you.'

The man and his wife began weeping and suddenly shook, just like I had been shaking that day (he confirmed that what I had said was true and realised God cared for him).

Several other words came; crystal clear word after word. What I remember about that crusade, what I really remember…is that it all happened as I pressed in to Him.

This lasted for five days and the presence of God came heavily, I longed for this every waking moment. I was changed by an insatiable desire for more of His presence, more than for food and water.

The Hebrides Islands is a diverse archipelago off the west coast of Scotland, the site of a massive revival in the 1940s and 50s. I was reading a detailed record of the revival that broke out on the Isle of Lewis, written by Colin and Mary Peckham. It was so intense and so encouraging that I flipped to the back to read more about the author. I saw there that he, Dr Colin Peckham, had listed his email address – so I decided to email him and see if he'd respond.

I really wanted to ask him, point blank, what caused revival. With his experience, he should be able to give me at least an opinion. So, I began the letter with an introduction of myself, a little bit of my history being raised in Zimbabwe and living in South Africa. I thought for a while and just wrote it out:

'In your experience, what is the secret to revival?'

I went on to another subject and hit 'send'.

I returned to reading, only to see that the book answered my bold question in the next chapter. It was plainly spelled out: the secret to revival is prayer. I marveled and nodded. It was truth because the Bible said it but I also knew it firsthand, having seen it with my own eyes. God pays attention to the prayers of his children. It says in 2 Chronicles 7:14,

'...if My people who are called by My name humble themselves and pray and seek My face and turn from their wicked ways, then I will hear from heaven, will forgive their sin and will heal their land.'

It is His promise that humble prayer is the answer.

I almost forgot about my email to Colin, which was very quick to get a response. He wrote back enthusiastically:

'I am South African myself! I was born and raised in Kwazulu Natal. I moved to Edinburgh, Scotland where I met my wife, a Gaelic speaking woman by the name of Mary Morrison. Now she is, of course Mary Peckham!'

He went on in his email, as if we were old friends. Then, at the end he wrote:

'By the way, the secret to revival is prayer.'

I smiled to myself. If only I had not asked that question – after all, the book answered it in the next chapter. I wrote back, explaining that I had moved on in the book and found the 'secret to revival' in the very next chapter. I thanked him for writing and decided to ask another question.

'I will be in Aberdeen, Scotland to visit with friends soon. Might I be so bold as to ask if I can come and visit you? I'd love to meet you in person!'

Again, his response was swift:

'Yes! Please come and visit us! I would love to welcome a fellow South African. We can have a dinner or afternoon together.'

I was elated.

Almost from the moment I arrived in Aberdeen to see Rick and Amy Brooks with City of Joy church, I anticipated the visit. I took Rick aside to share my excitement with him.

'Hey, have you heard of Dr Colin Peckham?'

Rick thought for a bit and answered, 'No, why?'

'Well, he's one of the writers of this book,' I handed Rick a copy of Sounds from Heaven, where Colin's name was on the cover. 'He's a subject matter expert on the Hebrides Revival and he's here at your doorstep in Edinburgh – only a three-hour drive away. Do you want to go?'

How could he refuse me? He must have seen the look in my eyes.

We packed into his car and drove to Edinburgh the next day. As soon as we walked into the Peckham house I could feel the pressure of tears at the back of my eyes. Mary came to the door and greeted us. When she spoke, I could not hold the tears back. I sat for an hour and a half after we got there, crying my eyes out. I couldn't speak - Rick and Amy and Callie did all of the talking (or asking questions) while I sat just crying and crying. No one seemed to be too concerned about me; they all knew I was being touched by the Holy Spirit. I left that place knowing that revival was still alive in their hearts and the residual spilled over to me (which is why I couldn't stop crying).

About four years later, Callie and I were going to Canada. We thought of seeing them and breaking our journey in Scotland, so I decided to write to Colin and ask if we could stay with them for three days. I considered my own question to be forward, but I knew he would say no if it was not good for him. I was delighted when he responded:

'Yes! Please come and stay with us. You can spend three days with us here in our home.'

They welcomed us like family. I got to see them in their community, their church and around each other. Colin had a double doctorate and was a very learned man but he never acted like a professor or doctor – he was incredibly humble.

Each morning at the breakfast table he sat down and asked if we could begin by reading the Bible. He would read it aloud, stopping and thinking about words in the passages, rolling them over in his mind. It was as if he had never read that passage before. It took a long time for him to make it through the portion he was reading, simply because he would chew it slowly. Callie and I were not impatient. It was a delight to see him this way. It was something about the way he read the Word – not as one would read a novel, it was as if he knew every word was living and he paid it respect by saying each one specifically, as though it had a right to be recognized.

Morning and evening when he would read the Bible and pray, we would weep. He held the Word up with such respect – it encouraged us to treat reading the Bible with renewed reverence.

Of course they told us stories of the revival. We drank in their sharing but mainly what I took away from those days with them were not their stories, but the way they truly valued God, His Word and His people. It was a place of love and honor and the presence of God was there because He was welcome.

They died recently; they will be greatly missed.

Therefore leaving the elementary teaching about the Christ, let us press on to maturity, not laying again a foundation of repentance from dead works and of faith toward God, of instruction about washings and laying on of hands, and the resurrection of the dead and eternal judgment and this we do if God permits

(Hebrews 6:1-3)

Knowing the basics of God's teaching is truly important to the Christian. The foundations of belief in Jesus Christ our cornerstone: repentance from dead works, faith, baptisms, laying on of hands, resurrection of the dead, and the coming judgment are non-negotiable in a believer's life. Like any good soldier knows; basic training is the beginning – but it's something you never forget. Forgetting our foundations is never an option – they are laid in our hearts like stones and on those stones our faith is built.

As I began to pursue God in the areas of revival and supernatural healing, I remembered this. I wanted to keep my faith alive and sharpened like a good sword but I also wanted to specialize, as a doctor specializes, in the power of the healing ministry. The more I pressed in and sought after Him, the more God was faithful to answer the desires of my heart. I wanted only to see Him glorified by seeing the lame walk, the blind see, the deaf hear…

The desire to be a vessel for His healing power dominated my prayer life and my reading list; I voraciously read books that reported true testimonies of divine healing. If God was the same yesterday, today and forever AND He couldn't lie, that meant He wanted to heal people miraculously today! The very thought excited me…

Apathy was not my nature. (A-Pathos, or 'without passion' is the Greek translation). I loved throwing myself into the fire of God. John Wesley is quoted as saying that preaching is the equivalent of setting yourself on fire and everyone around comes to watch you burn, – It's true! So I passionately pursued the healing gifts, the power of God's divine nature.

I read about great revivals happening and hungered for the same thing to happen at the meetings, in the outreaches and during crusades. I noticed that there were basically two types of leaders: the leaders whose prayers called for people's attendance, advertising budgets and a great turnout at the revival; and the leaders whose prayers called for GOD's PRESENCE at the revival.

It changed the way I hosted meetings.

I began to pray only for God's presence; it was no longer so important that my events were well attended. After all, if God was there, the people would come. I began to pray fervently for the presence to come and minister through me. I started to see change at every meeting – there was always a sense of HIS PRESENCE. Every time there were signs and wonders that would follow the meeting – a manifestation of HIS PRESENCE.

If there is not the response of the Lord after or in the meetings, then who have you talked about? When Callie talks about me, I want to be there and listen in. When I talk about her, she wants to be there and listen in. If God is being spoken of, He wants to be there. He loves to hear His children speaking about Him and it is His delight to listen in. It is His delight to move among His children. The Holy Spirit is attracted to His name.

When you give Him time, the Holy Spirit loves to move. He loves to show up and minister and make Himself known.

———

In 2013 Callie and I returned to Poland for the twelfth time. As usual, we travelled around to visit many churches. We had so many invitations that we would travel to a new place every night, sleeping in different beds every night we were there.

Our beloved brothers, the church pastors, set up meeting after meeting, knowing that I'd be ready for them and knowing that people would come. The first couple of times we were there God worked through us to bring His life and the people wanted more. There was also another thing that people liked about us (I found it strange that this would be a reason we would be asked back so many times). When I preached I didn't 'bash Catholicism' – a problem that pastors experienced with most evangelical speakers. Poland has a long Catholic history and the people are still sensitive when cruel things are said about their religion in the name of God. I learned early on not to destroy something in order to justify what I believed in.

We would preach Jesus- only Jesus. People there believed in divine healing and were desperate for it. People would drive a hundred kilometers just to be at a meeting where healing might take place. When word got out that there were physical and emotional (and psychological) healings taking place, the Poles would flock to our meetings, starving for God's touch.

I remember one morning in Radzyń Podlaski when an older man came into one of our meetings dressed in a three-piece suit and using a fancy walking stick. He looked very posh and I figured he thought he was coming to a denominational conference where suits and ties were required. He sat down, assisted by his daughter who had brought him. It was then I realized that this man actually used that walking stick as a cane; it wasn't for show. During the meeting I called out to anyone who needed divine healing to come forward. The man made his way to the front, assisted by his daughter.

Immediately, the Lord made it clear that this man didn't have any kind of faith at all. I greeted the man and asked, 'Do you know your healer?'

'That's you, isn't it?'

I said, 'No, it's not – it's Jesus Christ.'

The man shook his head, indicating he didn't. I turned to the pastor who led the church that was hosting the conference. 'Will you please lead this man to Jesus Christ? After he knows Him as Lord, he'll be able to meet Him as healer.'

The pastor stepped forward and began the ministry of salvation with the man. Meanwhile, there were flocks of people coming forward for physical healings. We prayed on and on that night- people were healed of many things; two I remembered were healed from scoliosis and a deaf ear was totally opened. There were multiple testimonies of physical healings and the church was encouraged and celebrating.

While all of this was going on, the old man came back to me. I recognized him and asked him, point-blank: 'Okay, do you know Jesus as Lord and Saviour now?'

'Yes, I do,' he answered, smiling.

'Do you receive Him as healer now? Because if you do, you will receive the other benefit of Him dying on the cross and that is a physical healing.'

The man agreed, enthusiastically. I knelt down in front of him and placed one hand on his hip and one on his knee. I prayed, I remember, a very simple prayer. It was no more than 'Lord, heal this man as You have promised.'

I stood up and the man seemed surprised that I was finished. I asked him to give me his walking stick and he did. Then I asked him, 'Do you see that aisle there? Do you think you can walk down that aisle and then walk back up again?'

The man looked over at the aisle in the middle of the church and then looked back at me. I was holding his walking stick and he didn't look so sure, but he walked away, determined to try. As he started to walk down the aisle he did so with care and caution but at some point he realized he wasn't hobbling or struggling. He started to walk faster and as he did, a spirit of celebration broke out all over him. He raised his hands in the air and started celebrating. Everyone in the church was cheering.

I love it when people respond with celebration! Sometimes I've prayed for people and they've been healed but they walk away as solemn as they came. You wonder if they realize what actually happened to them.

The man came back up the aisle, exuberant. I handed him back his walking stick as both he and his daughter thanked me profusely. I kept pointing upwards, meaning that it was God who did the healing, therefore, God who should be thanked.

The church continued in celebration. When it was time for the meeting to end, the old man was restless and still in a celebratory mood. He walked up to the pastor (obviously unfamiliar with the Christian mandate of sitting still in church and not being disruptive!) and handed him his walking stick.

'Here, take my stick!' he said. 'Take this thing! I don't need this anymore! Why would I need this?'

With that, the man strutted down the aisle of the church and into the fresh air. He was obviously off to enjoy the rest of his day.

On that very same trip to Poland, God healed many people. For some reason, it was like a fresh wind and rain was with us. God made himself known over and over again- too many times to count.

Near the end of the trip, we were invited into a new church and I remember a young woman who came forward for healing. She was only twenty-five or six, but she had a host of medical problems. 'What are you trusting God for today?' I asked her, as she came to the front.

'I was born blind in my right eye,' she told me. 'I haven't ever been able to see out of it. I also have swollen joints in my hands from arthritis…' She showed me her young hands, twisted and swollen knuckles that seemed to belong to someone much older. 'Do you see I can't take my rings off? I also have terrible back pain…'

Before she could go on about all of her ailments, I said: 'Well Jesus can heal all of those things! Which one do you want healing from first?'

She was surprized by my question, but answered, 'I want to see out of my eye.'

'Okay, it shall be done.' I put my hand over her right eye and began to pray. In a few minutes I finished praying and took my hand away; she covered her left eye and exclaimed, 'I can see your buttons!' She had been looking straight ahead at my shirt, so the first thing she saw were my buttons. I turned her around and covered her left eye with my hand.

'Tell me now what you see,' I asked her.

'I see a guy wearing a t-shirt in American writing,' she said. She read the writing out loud to me and I laughed with joy. The blind see? Thank you, God!

Since we were now full of faith, I asked what she wanted prayer for next. She was so excited she couldn't decide but finally blurted out that her back was still sore. What I didn't know was that this girl had a twisted spine, one that she had lived with for a long time.

The pastor of the church, one of his elders, the translator and I stood watching what the power of God was doing, Before our eyes (I had never seen this happen before) the girl grew! It was obvious that her spine was untwisting and straightening. The girl's smile was so big that I knew she knew what was going on. She began to shake and tremble by the power of God; her rings came unstuck as her hand swelling reduced dramatically. I watched the incredible power of God's healing on this ONE GIRL! Many healings going on in her body at once! It was astounding!

She stayed there, in the pure presence of God for about an hour, shaking and trembling under the power. It was an incredible time and I saw with my own eyes the undeniable physical healing of this girl.

I think (sadly) divine healing has been forgotten by the church. If it has not been forgotten, then it has been doubted. People are fearful to ask God to heal, and yet it is the greatest tool and weapon the church has for winning souls, changing nations and restoring passion to the church.

If I were to address the church at large, not one particular church, I would have to say there are a few final thoughts that I would share. I consider it a great honor to address the people of God and I don't take this lightly, so what I'm about to say has oceans of His grace all over it.

1. We need to know exactly why the Son of God came and what the works of the evil one are.

'The one who practices sin is of the devil; for the devil has sinned from the beginning. The Son of God appeared for this purpose, to destroy the works of the devil.' ~I John 3:8

What is the work of the evil one? To hold everyone in unbelief or doubt, as he did from the beginning in the Garden of Eden – with the GREAT LIE. He wants to question God's authority, or God's Word. The church's role today should be to bring everyone back to the truth of the Bible. Not a commentary on the Bible, not an opinion of what the Bible says, but THE BIBLE. The Good News of Jesus Christ is from Genesis to Revelation and we need to get back to the life-saving truth of the Bible.

When Jesus was tempted by the devil each time He answered, 'It is written.'

When it comes to the church, we leaders have a responsibility to read, preach, teach and live the Word of God in its entirety. When we leave out certain passages of the Bible, or ignore them, we ourselves become liars - part of the great lie. It's important that we meditate on the Word of God daily and allow it to wash over us. Many people are led astray by teachers who are preaching only portions of the Word of God because they themselves do not know it. I charge you – know the Son!

The devil wants to distract us, discourage us and derail our mission. We must remember that he is defeated and we need not be afraid of his lies.

2. We need to be baptized in the Holy Spirit to be anointed with His power.

> *'You know of Jesus of Nazareth, how God anointed Him with the Holy Spirit and with power, and how He went about doing good and healing all who were oppressed by the devil, for God was with Him.'* - Acts 10:30

We are baptized believers when we are dunked under water as a sign of the New Covenant. This happens after we have made a statement of faith in Jesus Christ as savior – but we need more.

We need to be anointed with the Holy Spirit and Power! It's more than just speaking in tongues, (which is important) we need God's power that comes with the baptism of the Holy Spirit!

The baptism of the Holy Spirit is for the purpose of receiving God's POWER for the ministry of the Kingdom. It says in Luke 24:49 that the disciples were told to stay put until they were "clothed with power from on high." Through this baptism we are empowered to go out into the nations (not get permission to go, God has already given us a mandate, we don't need permission) to bear witness to the Word of God and heal the sick. Jesus went out and did it before us and we are to do the same as He did. We need God's power to do this.

This brings me to what God says in 3 John 2: that we are to '…prosper and be in good health, just as your soul prospers.' Healing of the soul and healing of the body are so closely linked; and it is the work of the church to do these things together.

3. We need to return to the basics.

> *'All Scripture is inspired by God and profitable for teaching, for reproof, for correction, for training in righteousness; so that the man of God may be adequate, equipped for every good work.'* ~1 Timothy 3:16

I would charge pastors of churches, shepherds of God's people to preach these things: Salvation and divine healing, which go together like twins. Also, allow room in your meetings for the power gifts of the Holy Spirit. God is never afraid to come and walk amongst us if we give Him room!

The second coming of Jesus Christ in all of His glory and the resurrection from the dead are hardly ever preached from the pulpit. Are we worried that it's too harsh? It's the basis of our faith! Political correctness has diluted the doctrine. Hardly anyone preaches about hell anymore now, why is that? Hell is as real as heaven – it needs to be driven home to our congregations.

Basic doctrines need to be obeyed. If you don't obey them, you will be plucked off by the enemy. I knew one sniper in the Rhodesian army. There was only the need for one because he was so successful. He told me the secret to his success was that he lived his life by the basics of his training. May the same be said of all of us – our success is dependent on how we live our lives and how dependent we are on the basics of our faith.

4. We need to know our weapons.

'For this reason I remind you to fan into flame the gift of God, which is in you through the laying on of my hands, for God did not give us a spirit of fear but of love power and sound mind' ``

2 Timothy 1:6

In 2 Timothy 1:6, Paul tells Timothy to 'fan into flame' the gift of God. This word 'fan' (some versions say 'stir-up') is the Greek word 'revive'. It's the only time a charge for revival is given to an individual in the New Testament.

We are given a great invitation; it's up to us to fan or stir. The only way to equip the troops for battle is to call in veterans who are specialized in certain weapons. If I wanted to stir up revival, I would call in the one who knows all about it!

When I was in Llewellyn barracks, we had a Color-Sergeant named Higgins as our platoon commander. Our platoon outshone the others in our company. Why?

Color-Sergeant Higgins was Special Forces NCO – a professional; he was in the elite SAS. He knew exactly what a good soldier was supposed to look like; he was one and expected us to be the same.

He never raised his voice at us except to command or give orders; we were never personally insulted. He knew from experience what worked and this is what he taught us.

So it is with the church. The fivefold ministries are like the five fingers on God's hand – there to equip the church. Rookies are little more than wannabe's and can only tell shallow stories. There is great value in being seasoned and 'blooded' in battle. While we can be youth-centric, I pray that we do not dismiss the need for seasoned professionals!

Arise generals! Know your weapons, saints! Leaders show yourselves approved and then come and teach the church how it is.

5. Make a record of your ministry, just to see what God has done.

For as long as I can remember I have kept a journal of God's goodness in the ministry. I have pages of healing after healing after healing that testify of God's power and righteous ability to heal. I have also kept a record of failures and pains.

He is the same yesterday, today and forever. He doesn't slumber nor does He sleep. There will always be many examples of His goodness that follow you. In the darkest times, you can return to that account and remember that He called you and you are partnering with Him.

A journal cannot be argued with – it is an account of Jesus. His goodness is alive and well among us. Don't miss the opportunity to chronicle what He is doing for future generations.

6. Get READY!

As I said earlier, I have decided to become a specialist in the area of divine healing and revival. I press in, read books and glean from others who have the same calling. I try to remain as teachable as I can so that I can always feel the wind of the Holy Spirit moving in the trees.

In addition to this, Callie and I feel the incredible desire and charge to pass on the baton to the younger generation who are running with us. I have no desire to build a ministry where I am the center – it's all about Jesus at the center and a lot of us with Him. The more I can train up the next generation and pass on what I have through impartation, the more reward I have.

There's no way I'll ever stop doing crusades; it's my passion and my love. But I want to pass the baton to someone who could take it at a moment's notice; someone who is ready in minutes to go out and make it happen.

I want to see old time camp meetings come back, where thousands gather for around the clock adoration, all of us worshipping our King together! I want to see divine healing and revivals going on in the camp meetings.

I want to see Ephesians 4:11-12 ministries operating at the same meetings, unthreatened by each other, tag-teaming, for up to three weeks, morning and evening, in tents equipping the saints, by not talking but demonstrating. This is REVIVAL.

How can we let 'church' be once a week when our savior, healer, Lord and God never sleeps? How did that come about? I want to run alongside of Him every day of the week.

Get up, church! AWAKEN! Let's do this thing.

A road in the wilderness - the future, the best is yet to come!

EPILOGUE: PRAY FOR ME

Pray also for me, that whenever I open my mouth, words may be given me so that I will fearlessly make known the mystery of the gospel, for which I am an ambassador in chains. Pray that I may declare it fearlessly, as I should.

Ephesians. 6:19, 20

I have given you only pieces of my story in the hopes that I may do only one thing: testify of Jesus and the power of His transforming love.

I have hoped to encourage you, dear reader, in your walk with God. I have also hoped to reflect the glory of the living God.

Because we get so many queries, Callie and I are happy to give you the information link to our website: www.keirtayler.com . There you will find testimonies, devotionals and a calendar of upcoming events

IF YOU ARE CURIOUS ABOUT OUR CHILDREN...

By the grace of God I have been given the most incredible children who are all adults now. When I started to put my book together, a friend suggested that our son and daughters might want to say something. Their contributions to this book (their love and support in the words you are about to read) have disarmed me.

I am so blessed.

~ *Keir*

Noble Fatherhood gives us a Glimpse of the Divine

Jenni Lloyd - *Johannesburg, Gauteng, South Africa*

My Dad was always present – he was at every gala, athletics day and hockey match he could be at. He taught me valuable life lessons and it is these values I learnt mainly from watching their lives – both my Dad and my Mum are epic examples of this. He introduced me to the greatest book ever – the Bible; he taught me that the call of God was what mattered, and yet never abandoned his family along the way, but rather took us with him as he pursued this. There were often times I did not understand why he had to go and leave us behind for periods of time, but I also understood that souls were so precious to Father God and I knew that while he was not present, God was with us all no matter where we lived or how far apart we were from him.

There is no such thing as a perfect parent, but there are great parents and he is a great Dad. He has always pointed me to Jesus – when he has felt a failure and incompetent, he showed me how perfect our heavenly Father is. He has loved me unconditionally, he has challenged me and has allowed me to grow which has often meant not rescuing me from hardship, but praying and standing with me. Despite the fact that I now have my own family and am 'grown up', I still like to 'bounce' things off him and get his wisdom and perspective – his opinions still count!

Being the oldest of three children, I was often the 'security' for my younger siblings when my parents travelled. I am naturally responsible and so whether right or wrong, I took it upon myself to care for them and kind of 'step in' when the folks were away. Simon and Lisa, in their younger years, could not stay with anyone unless I was with them. I fiercely protected them and loved them. I guess this was also preparation for my family one day.

As I was a 'PK' (Pastors Kid), there were life experiences that I was exposed to. For me, it was my life and I knew no other. There were, however, certain expectations that sadly people placed on us as pastor's kids. Although I do believe in being a good example, it was the 'call of God' on us as a family that people sometimes did not fully understand. I did see a lot more than I probably should have but thankfully church politics, people and the ministry did not deter me from loving and serving my Heavenly Father. My Dad was enabled to do what he did because of the 'unsung hero' in our family – my mother. She gave him complete freedom to pursue the call and at the same time raised a young family and, for the most part, we lived far away from loved ones and family. Now as a mother, I fully understand that sacrifice and know that it was only God's grace, and her commitment to serving Him that allowed us to continue on in what He had for us as a family.

Some memories that are etched in my mind are my Dad teaching me certain Proverbs in the afternoon while we 'acted out the scriptures'. Another is him helping me at the age of eight to learn my times tables (which I am forever grateful for). He helped me learn discipline in studying and setting goals both in school and in life.

He walked me down the aisle and 'gave' me away and then performed the ceremony. I dedicated the song 'Butterfly Kisses' and we all cried (and still do when we hear it). He was there to dedicate my children to God – and is always cheering us on as we walk the road of parenthood. How rich I am!!

There is a famous saying, 'That anyone can be a Father, but not everyone is a Dad' – Dads are incredibly special to sons and daughters. To sons, they are their first hero, and to daughters, their first love! Apparently they often say that daughters choose husbands who have certain character traits or interests or similarities to their own fathers. It is because of a great role model in my Dad that I chose and looked for similar strengths in my husband, such as integrity, honesty, strength, courage and faithfulness.   *~Jenni*

Consistently Passionate

Simon Tayler - *Ballito, Kwa-Zulu Natal, South Africa*

One of the earliest memories I have is of my father reading Bible stories to my older sister and I on the floor of our home in Zimbabwe. He was always my hero: big, strong, adventurous and passionate. My parents laid a foundation rooted deep in the Word. As children we were often exposed to more than most children were. I remember attending an open church service for the employees on a family friend's farm. I saw my first demon manifest right there and observed as the calm authority of Christ was demonstrated through my father as he told it to leave. The pastor of the 'church' then proceeded to take an offering and gave it all to me. I was immediately humbled by the generosity and went with my parents to pick out my first Bible the next day.

Growing up in the church I got to witness many styles of leadership and pastoring. I got to witness God's hands on our lives and His faithfulness to those who are obedient and passionately seek Him at all costs. My parents were amongst the few who, no matter how difficult times got, passionately pursued His Kingdom.

My parents lead us by example with a firm but gentle hand. I was the rebellious child in the family and often wandered off the straight and narrow. My parents always pointed and never pushed me to Jesus. It was through faithful prayer and consistent love and encouragement that I came back to Jesus and ignited a love for His church.

My father is gentle, loving, encouraging and steadfast; but most of all he is consistently passionate about the Kingdom and everyone experiencing HIM - most of all his children. My mother is generous, caring and supportive. She is supportive and faithful in all circumstances and is always encouraging.

Our lives, as a family, are anything but ordinary thanks to extra-ordinary parents who would sacrifice all to see His Kingdom come. They have truly taught me what it is to Love like the Father and serve Him wholeheartedly. No greater gift could ever be bestowed upon a child.

Thank you Dad & Mum   *~Simon*

GO and See Something or Stay and See Nothing

Lisa Haynes - *Redding, California USA*

I grew up falling asleep under the chairs in church meetings; going to Sunday school every week and knowing my dad was a missionary into Mozambique. I grew up singing songs in church about seeking God's Kingdom and going on adventures with God and laying down my life for Jesus. I would watch my dad leave on his motorbike with his Bible and backpack and arrive back home ten days later; glowing as he would tell us story after story about healing, salvations and miracles.

At the age of five I asked my mom to pray with me as I gave my heart to Jesus. And at the age of fourteen I met God in the middle of the Mozambique bush.

For the first time I saw God's raw power touch those who didn't know what church was and had only heard the name of Jesus once. I saw Him love people who were broken, diseased and hopeless. I saw Him heal the sick and deliver the tormented. No boxes, no rules. Nothing but Love in Action. I made a decision that evening while my dad preached to the noisy crowd in the bush. I made a decision to give everything I have and ever will have for His Kingdom; for Him. Sixteen years later my heart still burns for Him.

My dad taught me how to love God's word, he drew me pictures as he illustrated the verses in the Bible. He taught me to take risks, to GO and see rather than stay and see nothing. He taught me to trust the Holy Spirit and to put action to faith. He tucked me in at night, made me laugh and took me to my horse riding lessons. He helped me study for my exams and made me scrambled eggs in the mornings.

My mom is the most beautiful and incredible woman I know. She taught me to lay down my life for the call of God. She showed me how to love others, how to give in times of need and how to worship in times of heartache. My mom believed in me more than I believed in myself. As a little girl I went everywhere with my mom. My dad travelled a lot and not once did I hear my mom complain about 'being left behind with the kids'. She understood her call to be a mother - the greatest call of all in my opinion. She is a mother to so many, not just her own. I am a mother now and I see the fruit of the seeds she has sown.

Being the baby of the family, I grew up being loved and supported. I have two older siblings who are my heroes. My sister is one of the strongest and deepest women I know. My brother is a leader and the most incredibly talented and genuine man.

I knew my family life wasn't 'normal' by worldly standards, but in my heart I knew this was what life and family was actually about. Kingdom is family, and family seeks the Kingdom.   *~ LIsa*

RECOMMENDED READING

Many of you have asked me for a recommended reading list (besides the Bible, which should be in a reachable place at all times). It is important to tell you to be a BEREAN as you read any book. When I read, I have a pen and I underline and make notes several times. I really dive into a book when I read it.

Great classics on Divine Healing:

1. **Divine Healing by Andrew Murray**
   Available here on Kalahari.net:

   http://www.kalahari.com/Books/Divine-Healing_p_29176157

   Available here on Amazon.com:

   http://www.amazon.com/Divine-Healing-Andrew-Murray/dp/0883681129/ref=sr_1_1?ie=UTF8&qid=1406767649&sr=8-1&keywords=divine+healing+andrew+murray

2. **The Ministry of Healing by A.J. Gordon**
   Available here on Kalahari.net

   http://www.kalahari.com/Books/The-Ministry-of-Healing-Miracles-of-Cure-in-All-Ages_p_43637534

   Available here on amazon.com:

   http://www.amazon.com/Ministry-Healing-Miracles-Classic-Reprint/dp/B0094XUUOK/ref=sr_1_1?s=books&ie=UTF8&qid=1406767823&sr=1-1&keywords=the+ministry+of+healing+a.j.+gordon

3. **The Gospel of Healing by A. B. Simpson**

    (In Africa ask for it at your local Christian bookseller –
    they can order it)

    Available here on amazon.com:

    http://www.amazon.com/Gospel-Healing-B-Simp-
    son/dp/1494340178/ref=sr_1_1?s=books&ie=UT-
    F8&qid=1406768083&sr=1-1&keywords=The+Gospel+of+Heal-
    ing+by+A.+B.+Simpson

4. **Christ the Healer by F.F. Bosworth**

    ISBN 978-0-8007-9457-6

    Available here on Kalahari.net:

    http://www.kalahari.com/Books/Christ-the-
    Healer_p_32733516

    Available here on Amazon.com:

    http://www.amazon.com/F.-F.-Bosworth/e/B001JSBSH6/
    ref=sr_ntt_srch_lnk_1?qid=1406768332&sr=1-1

5. **Healing the Sick by T.L. Osborn**

    ISBN: 0-89274-403-0

    Available here on Kalahari.net:

    http://www.kalahari.com/Books/Healing-the-Sick_p_591290

    Available here on amazon.com:

    http://www.amazon.com/Healing-Sick-T-L-Osborn/
    dp/0892744030/ref=sr_1_1?s=books&ie=UT-
    F8&qid=1406769014&sr=1-1&keywords=Healing+the+Sick+by
    +T.+L.+Osborn

Other Compelling Books:

God's Generals by Roberts Liardon
ISBN: 978-1-60374-090-6

Available here on Kalahari.net:

http://www.kalahari.com/Books/God-s-Generals_p_39260622

Available here on Amazon.com:

http://www.amazon.com/Gods-Generals-They-Succeed-ed-Some/dp/0883689448/ref=sr_1_1?s=books&ie=UT-F8&qid=1406768584&sr=1-1&keywords=god%27s+gener-als+by+roberts+liardon

Sounds from Heaven (The Revival on the Isle of Lewis 1948-1952) by Colin and Mary Peckham
ISBN 1-85792-953-5

Available here from Kalahari.net:

http://www.kalahari.com/Books/Sounds-from-Heav-en_p_27903018

Available here from Amazon.com:

http://www.amazon.com/Sounds-Heaven-Reviv-al-1949-1952-Biography/dp/1857929535/ref=sr_1_1?s=-books&ie=UTF8&qid=1406768864&sr=1-1&keywords=-sounds+from+heaven

Secrets of Authority by Andrew Murray
ISBN-10: 0-88368-853-0

Available here on Kalahari.net

http://www.kalahari.com/Books/Secrets-of-Authori-ty_p_27215940

Available here on amazon.com:

http://www.amazon.com/Secrets-Authority-Andrew-Murray/dp/0883688530/ref=sr_1_1?ie=UTF8&qid=1406769179&s-r=8-1&keywords=secrets+of+authority+murray

ACKNOWLEDGEMENTS

This book is but a reflection of my life, but embraces more lives that are silent in the pages. Firstly, my wife, intimate friend, partner and mother of my children; Callie, you have been the most amazing person I have ever known. I have sat, watched and marveled over you more than any other person. Your silent strength, compassion, and understanding are mirrored in your beautiful blue eyes. You have watched me drive off into the known and unknown on many occasions. The war days were pure devotion to our love for each other with a never spoken understanding that I might never return. You managed our home, and children in my absence 'on mission'. You have shared the pains and struggles in ministry, in crossing borders, making a house into a home on many occasions. You have been a devoted wife and loving mother. You have travelled with me into many nations, stood with me on platforms and loved the people. You totally complete me.

Also, my three amazing children – Jenni, Simon and Lisa. You often lay in bed at night knowing 'Dad's away again', knowing in your young hearts that this was the call of God on all of our lives. Now by the gracious hand of God you understand and are walking in your inheritance. Thank you for being patient, enduring the vacuums and yet loving our God so much. You married partners who were handpicked by God and know this calling: Michael, Peter and Nicole, I want to thank you for loving our children uncon-ditionally and giving us our beautiful grandchildren; Mikaela, Conor, Starla, Levi and Tayla Lloyd – Nathan and Sean Tayler – Amy and Katie Haynes.

My Dad, Harry who went through Dartmouth Naval College and WW2, whose discipline and humor massively shaped my life. My mother, Monica, a true pioneer in Africa, your compassion and patience has left a mark.

To all our friends who have regularly encouraged Callie and I to 'write a book'. Voila!

My Selous Scout buddies - with whom I shared many scary moments with and who were always there when most needed. Two soldiers I will never forget: Major Higgins (Brit. SAS), and Master Sgt Lorry Mc Gorian (US Ma-rines). They were experienced, exceptional and deeply influenced my life as a young trooper. Pastor Jim Hodges at CFNI; as both tutor and Pastor. Dr. Rodney Howard-Browne. Dr. Edwin Louis Cole. Dudley Daniel. Dr. Colin Peckham and many who I have never met, but whose books have shaped faith, values and vision.

Janet Rodriguez who has penned these pages and made it happen. Martha Dayton for your graphics, design and publishing.